The Blood Orange Tree
Poems and Stories
by
M Crane Hana

The Blood Orange Tree

M. Crane Hana

Published by Crane Hana Books, 2020.

THE BLOOD ORANGE TREE

First edition. November 21, 2020.

ISBN: 979-8227073921

Written by M. Crane Hana.

Table of Contents

Dedication

For the family and friends who not only put up with a writer and artist in their lives, but a writer and artist *like me*. My deep thanks for your tolerance, and many apologies for the inconvenience.

Like it or not, many authors are influenced by their environments. I'm no different. This collection, while it has fantasy and science fiction elements, is primarily an ode to the landscapes and often-conflicting cultures of the American Southwest...specifically, New Mexico and Arizona. This land is the reason why my instinctive artist's default colorway is turquoise, rust, and yellow ochre: the skies and hills I opened my eyes to over fifty years ago.

Author's note: the dates after the titles mark completion dates for the first versions of each piece. Given my tendency to revise and rewrite, that could be a decade or two before the final version.

AO3-style warning tags: grief, loss, deception, obsession, unreliable narrators, climate change.

Four Hours

2004

Four hours out of twenty-four
Flank midnight, dusk, noon, and dawn.
Ancient rhythms coded deep
Govern minds awake, asleep,
Force our lives to hurry on.
Our days are sliced to frantic hours
Yet within them wait elusive powers
To stir or bless, calm or cure.
Array your time to breathe a breeze
Or grant a tree a second look.
Allow a moment's rest to please
As you linger with this book.

Guiding Angels

2013

I have no guardian angels.
My guiding angels are not
Domestic spirits
Or jealous seraphim.
They are weak forces
Strong forces
Gravity
Foundations of broken symmetry
And the longing of the universe
To know itself.

The Blood Orange Tree

1989

Who runs out of gasoline three days in a row in the same place, in the Arizona desert?

The first morning I drove on, and felt guilty the rest of the day. The second morning I imagined a murderer's van lurking behind the mesquite groves just off the highway. The third morning, I saw the same weary young figure trudging past the same milepost, a gasoline can banging his knees as he walked. How would I feel in his place? I stopped on the shoulder, and rolled down my window as I watched him hurry to meet the car. "Where are you headed?"

He glanced toward the south. "Into the city."

"Car break down?"

"Motorcycle. A few miles back." He waved his free hand toward the northwest. "Thanks for stopping, lady."

When Phoenix teens his age said 'lady' it meant 'forty-something fat bitch'. His 'lady' was different enough that I said, "Join me and Grey Mare, then."

He bent to look through the window. "You have a horse?"

"The Saab." I patted the dashboard. "From a Tolkien story with an old grey mare of uncommon good sense."

"Ah," he said. "Sympathetic magic."

I reminded him about the seatbelt. He fumbled with the catch, and jumped at the Mare's stuttering engine. I smiled. He turned to look out the window.

Jackrabbits and mourning doves watched us pass. A hawk soared high enough to be gilt by dawn-light. The boy frowned at the hawk.

When the road let me, I glanced at him. Sixteen, I thought, maybe seventeen. Old enough to snarl if I accidentally called him a 'boy' to his face. Thin, tall, colt-knobby at the joints. Bronze-red hair curled against high cheekbones and olive skin. Jeans dark and crisp, a clean grey T-shirt, a storm-blue jacket with the sheen of silk. He didn't smell of three days in the desert, or even an hour. I didn't think the jacket hid a gun.

On the floor, the gasoline can rocked. Red-orange dust stained the boy's jeans. I saw the other side of the can, its metal a pitted lacework of rust.

The Mare jittered over the center line.

My knuckles whitened on the steering wheel. I kept my voice light. "You've been here three days. What do you want?"

"Help me. Before sunrise."

A juvenile detention center, heralded by Do Not Stop For Hitchhikers signs, lay not too many miles eastward. More sunlit hawks wheeled over a salt flat ahead. "What happens at sunrise?"

"To you? Nothing. Will you take me into the city?"

I glanced east. The first sliver of sunlight pierced a gap in the mountains. Half a mile before us, mirages rippled golden above asphalt. "Please?" he whispered, staring ahead, his fingers clenching the seatbelt. "All right." Why not? "To the city."

Peach-golden light spilled across the desert and into my car. The boy cast a watery shadow against torn upholstery. He forced one hand against his lips. A hawk dipped by my side window, pacing the car, its wingtip almost brushing the glass. Over the Mare's engine, I heard the hawk's scream recede into distance.

Sunlight. The hawk was gone.

When I glanced over, the boy's shadow was solid as mine. His smile was unsteady, his grey eyes bright. "Thank you," he said.

"You're welcome. Just send some luck my way."

"On my honor, I will."

Such words. Prep school? Royalty?

"So," I said, "Your motorcycle ran out of gas three mornings in a row."

"And somebody stole my real gas can today, about ten miles before that town..."

"Wickenburg. Better make that twenty miles. I live ten miles north of it."

"Twenty, then."

"Why are you afraid of dawn? Why are you here?"

"Oranges."

"Oranges?"

"My father owns an experimental nursery in, er, Nevada. Hybridizing plants to arid regions. Grafting delicate strains to strong stock. He sent me down to look at an odd old variety he wants, growing at a private ranch. I'll try to buy some cuttings. Our orchards are dying out. This hybrid might save them."

The mile markers surged by. I began to wonder about our game. "I know legends about oranges."

He humored me. "Really?"

"The golden apples of the Hesperides. One of Hercules' tasks, I think. A 17th Century Dutchman said they were oranges. Maybe the Hebrew's Tree of Knowledge was an orange tree. Or was it apricot? And I read a fantasy book once, long ago, that said every thirteenth fruit of the orange tree held a wish. They were only folktales, but beautiful."

"You're a scholar?"

"Hardly. My family lived in a good part of Phoenix. The houses seemed to come with their own transplanted English gardens. Whoever designed ours was a citrus addict. He'd left his books in the attic."

The regal voice sharpened. "Those books. Do you own them still?"

"My mother sold them in an estate sale years ago. To help me pay for art school. For all the good it did us, we should have kept the books and the house."

"I smelled orchards blooming before dawn. I thought the city was magical at night, from up in the mountains," the boy said. "A lake of stars."

"Most of the orchards are pastel subdivisions by now. It's only February. Right now, you smell the old orange trees in yards and along the freeways. The green doesn't really belong here. Like the swimming pools and golf courses. Phoenix is as much a mirage as Vegas."

"Vegas?"

"Never mind." I wondered where he really lived.

"I wish you could see it through my eyes, lady."

"I can't see around the past."

"What past?" His hand flattened on my forehead.

"Oh," I said.

The Arizona Tourism Board must marshal legions of photographers on mornings like this, I thought. Twenty miles away, skyscrapers rose like crystal blocks. Surreal mountains ringed the city, speared up through it in seven-hundred-foot-high scarps of russet and amber sandstone. Golf courses and swimming pools were beryls and sapphires set in a misty golden valley. The abomination was beautiful because it had no right to exist, an ephemeral kingdom made as much of illusion as water and steel.

"Treasure it. It cannot last," he whispered. His fingertips left my skin, but some of the sudden magic stayed. "I know deserts. This one waits below the surface to once more devour its lands. The desert says people lived here long ago, and it did the same to them. Who were they?"

"Hohokam," I dredged up high-school memories. "Native Americans. Canal-builders. Some of the new canals follow the old channels. They're long gone. Some of the nearby tribes are descendants."

The boy nodded. "Whoever rebuilt those canals made the same bargain as before, probably unwitting. The desert's magic, in exchange for desolation later. Whatever lives and grows here has the power to defy time and entropy, at least for a while."

"This is just Phoenix."

This is *Phoenix*, lady. A city twice-risen from sand, called after the Benu, the Firebird? There is great power in names. Anything can happen here, while the city stands and water flows through it."

"You're nuts."

"You're blind."

"Perhaps, but I'm the driver."

"Then watch where you're going."

The surviving citrus orchards yielded to pink-walled, fake-adobe subdivisions and seedy strip malls. The painterly part of my brain stopped its habitual self-doubt long enough to piece together a sketch. Under a hot white noon sky, three orange-tree dryads danced in a desert full of shattered glass and metal. Their bodies were lush, heavy as mine, relics of a beauty centuries out of style. I had never thought of myself as beautiful, but the dryads were. I tried to analyze the imagery. A manifesto railing against over-development? A 20th century take on Classicism? A size-wise fairy tale?

The vision refused explanation.

"Where are we going?" asked my passenger, pulling me out of the reverie in time to realize I'd been pacing traffic at an effortless seventy miles per hour, instead of my normal plodding fifty-five.

"I work downtown. Where do you need to be?"

"Are you a painter there?"

"I wish. I don't even know what art is, anymore. Did you know, there's a guy in London who makes art from dead sharks and cows in formaldehyde tanks?"

He made a disgusted noise. "We have people like that, too. Are they valued here?"

"Enough to be famous for a while. The recession hit even him in the end, I guess. My day-job is desk jockey for an information security company. I keep telling myself I'm only waiting for the big break. Let's worry about your future, first. The bus connections aren't the best. But they'll get you close to your orange tree. Do you know the address?"

"Bus?" he asked.

I was late to work, giving him cash to buy an all-day transit pass. I planned another painting during my mid-morning break: in brownish purple dusk, a scene of tropical fish swimming between wire fences and cacti. I imagined city lights blooming down in a valley, like lost Atlantis in an undersea rift.

Like the dryads it refused agenda, craving only existence.

I pushed my last sketch aside and concentrated on work. Downtown Phoenix intruded through the window. By late afternoon, an unfamiliar city rebuilt itself outside the office window: all angles, color-washed planes, clean lines that echoed back to a 1920's ideal of glorified technology and a bright future.

So many ideas. Could I paint even one of them? Trying would cost me nothing but the old watercolor paints slowly drying in their tubes. Blank paper waited in my tiny studio, a dozen white-shuttered windows that didn't need reasons or markets or clients to exist.

I walked outside to the Mare.

Go home right now, sang the sun and the wind in the green palm-fronds, *and you can paint whatever you want as long as you live.*

I saw the boy leaning against my car, his head bent over his hands. The lines of his body, outlined by red-orange sunlight, almost made me reach for the little sketchbook in my purse.

"Any luck?"

He looked up, face set in a scowl. "No. I need your help again."

The muse's moment began to ebb. I might still paint. If I got in the Mare without involving myself again. The orange-tree dryads, the desert reef, and the crystal towers begged me to drive away.

"The owner wasn't cooperative," he snarled. He tossed away the object in his hands, a dead brown twig shedding desiccated leaves. "He wanted things I didn't have. Credit cards, check guarantee cards, my father's tax number, references. And he wouldn't take what I had for payment! All for a wretched, half-dead tree that no one will be able to save in a few years!"

My moment of perfect creativity fled. "What did you try to give him? Not the gasoline can, I hope."

He upended a fist-sized bag on the Mare's hood. I winced at the noise, then forgot to breathe.

Finger-long bars of reddish gold, chased with wavy interlocking designs, clanged against old steel. Polished gemstone nuggets caught the sun, flaring Gulf-stream blue, dark carmine, jungle-green. A perfect spectrum sprayed across pitted paint, from a water-clear stone the diameter of my thumb.

The boy glared at the trove. "He said I was probably a thief. Then he threw me out. Threatened to call the police. So I found you again."

I leaned back against my car. "How on earth?" Did I really want to know how he found me, in all of central Phoenix? "What now?"

"You helped me once." He scooped up a handful of gems and gold. "You're poor, but you know this city. You can turn this trash into useful coin. It's yours."

"If I can get you back to that ranch tonight."

"Yes."

If I couldn't paint, I thought, I might as well try being rich and talentless.

We idled along quiet drives curtained in the deep greens made possible by water and money. I saw too many short-sale signs in front of the sprawling houses on this rich street. "We may be just in time," I said. "Your farmer might sell to a real-estate investor, if he's not losing his property to a bank."

"Would the new owners keep the orchard?"

"Maybe some of the younger, prettier trees."

We drove past the orchard and its high iron gates. While my passenger chewed his fingernails, I parked half a block away. "No for-sale sign," I said. "He's fighting the tide and staying. That means he'll have security."

"I'll get you out of it."

"I suppose you'll flash gold in front of the guards?"

"No guards. Just sizzling wires and tiny lights."

"Electronics, then," I sighed.

"I didn't come this far to let a fence stop me."

And I hadn't come this far to stay with the Mare.

The boy ghosted to the main gate. I expected him to have tools. Then again, remembering

golden bars, I wasn't startled when he simply raised a hand to the iron. Something crackled. I smelled acrid smoke. The gate swung open. All the nearby crickets stopped chirping.

"Come on," he whispered. "I'll need your help inside."

I followed him, my sensible heels catching on twigs but making little sound. Black shapes loomed ten or fifteen feet from the floor of the night, the orchard an alien labyrinth. Peacocks shrieked in the distance. Tree branches drooped, offering leafy boughs and thorns, sweet fruit and rancid windfalls, scent shifting between early blossoms and winter decay.

Coppery sodium-vapor light, reflected from ragged clouds overhead, limned a clearing occupied by one weathered shed and a tree. I saw the root stock, its few crooked stems carrying stunted, nearly-fossilized brown globes. From that dreary nest lifted a smooth grey trunk shrouded in waxy leaves, fruited in golden constellations.

The main tree, the scion. A dwarf Yggdrasil? A Tsarina's Faberge toy? It should flourish jade leaves and moonstone blossoms, its silver trunk springing from a golden urn in a museum.

The next glance showed me brown edges and yellowed leaves. Even dying, this tree flung out desperate attempts at new life.

"What now?" I whispered.

"Start the count. You pick where."

I considered one heavy fruit among many. An orange. Unmysterious. I could buy its cousin at any grocery. But I remembered childhood and hand-colored books: Eve's apple, Hellenic myths, Arabian Nights tales of forbidden orchards.

Another dour medieval legend surfaced: "I can't," I said. "Women supposedly blighted orange trees with a single touch."

"Are you a virgin, then?"

"Watch your mouth! I went to college."

"And you remember it?"

"Sadly, yes."

"We'll risk it. Have you gloves?"

I saw his grin, in the copper light. "Gloves, he wants," I told the tree.

"We'll need a lawyer if we get caught."

"For an orange or two? From necromancers who put pickled animals on pedestals? What a world you live in. Choose, lady."

I pointed into the dark green void at one fruit. No different than its fellows. Merely the first my eyes found. "That one."

He pointed from that to the next, whispering each number until..."Thirteen!"

He snapped the last orange from its twig with a tiny snick. He tucked the fruit into his jacket.

Then he reached up and snagged my orange. "Here. They're blood oranges. You can't find them often in the markets you frequent, I'd guess. Your wage." The easy arrogance in his voice stung me, did not sting me at all. The strong, clean citrus smell was worth that much.

A tardy alarm shrilled near the main house. We'd left the gate open. A sensor woke. Lights stuttered on. Peacocks wailed. I heard a man's voice raised in question.

We ran. Like Cinderella, I lost a shoe on the way. The boy darted through the gate. As I passed, it brushed my arm and bestowed a kissing shock. But the Mare waited, her ignition blessedly loyal. While flashlights still stabbed through the dark orchard, we rocketed away, laughing like fools.

No one followed us. I stopped in a parking lot between an all-night taqueria and a grocery store. Untrimmed palm trees edged the street, their papery brown fronds creaking. In the parking lot, low-riders whooped and made their cars buck to music.

The boy dug out a knife from his jacket and began to peel his prize.

"What about your father?"

"He wanted the cuttings to renew our orchards. He said the ripe fruit was useless unless it had grown from our soil. I don't see why. One orange might spawn more trees from its seeds than one cutting."

"No," I said, remembering the citrus addict's books. "Cross-pollination. The tree bloomed in that orchard with other oranges. There are still thousands of citrus trees in this valley. God knows what you'd get from the seeds. Only a cutting would grow true to the strain."

His knife trembled across the orange's pitted skin, stopped in mid-cut. He looked back at me, then out across the city. He smiled.

"No." I made it final by turning off the Mare's engine. "We are not going back."

"No, we're not. I don't need to."

"Your land. Your father?"

My companion shrugged. "I thought I had failed. But if I stay here, I haven't. The cuttings were for my people, and I'm not sure I want to walk among them again. But this orange? This is for me."

"All this for an orange?"

He gave me the knife hilt-first in a courtly flourish. "For this orange, yes. Try yours."

I held mine untouched in my other hand, and watched him.

He peeled thirteen sections away from the pith. The boy bit into the first wedge, trailing white membranes from the nipped edge. The dark-red, shredded pulp vesicles looked more like organ meat than fruit. "Not hungry?" he teased.

I felt like a drunk teenager on a dare. One wish. Love or talent? Or wealth, which might buy facsimiles of both? A better life, certainly. It wouldn't be wrong to eat this orange. Only wasteful. I might never paint again. But I'd never forget how I'd felt, in that sunset moment when I could paint whatever I chose. And let lapse the gift to help a stranger.

"I'll keep it." I handed back the knife. "How is yours?"

"Beautiful."

In the brief, silken silence I remembered the day's embryonic pictures. If I reached for them, they'd vanish. Remembering them was torment. Forgetting them, unthinkable.

The boy tucked twelve orange segments into his jacket, then opened the car door.

"Where are you going?"

"To find real magic. The kind you have, lady. There's more power here than in any place I know, and I want it. Thank you for showing it to me." He leaned over and kissed me briefly on the lips. Nothing else. The scent of the orchard rose from his hair and skin.

"How will you get back to—to Nevada?" I asked, as the secondhand taste of the wishing-orange stung on my lips, the tip of my tongue.

"Who cares? I'd rather see this world first." He set the treasure bag on the passenger's seat. Then he walked away from the Mare.

"Wait!"

Some of the low-riders looked over and laughed, not cruelly, at a plain, heavy, middle-aged woman calling after some jail-bait hustler. The boy didn't look back. The palm-fronds closed behind him.

"You can't survive here," I began. "Oh, hell." How would I even report him to the police?

Who'd believe me? I looked at the top half of my face in the rear-view mirror. A data-entry clerk. A non-entity who thought she was an artist. Whose paintings died stillborn between mind and canvas.

I still smelled him and the orange.

Who started trends, I wondered, warming my orange in my hands. The wise, the powerful, the unconventional, the fearless, and the frightening. Maybe I should be grateful, for being last compared to a pickled shark. But today I'd seen dreams that deserved to be painted, whether I sold them or not.

"I can try," I said to the orange. "I can *do*."

A Cadillac backfired, in tempo to a Latino cover of a Duran Duran song. I jumped, then laughed, and wiped a few decades of useless tears from my eyes. When I looked up again, I saw neon signs, glossy automobiles, and jeans-clad dancers. Women laughing. Men making love to women in a roundabout way, their cars dancing like courting birds of paradise. I saw joy. And I saw, finally, how to paint it.

The muse wasn't a moment, but a mindset. As long as I remembered how those moments felt, the swirling possibilitied became real enough to see, to paint.

I felt the muse's moment stretch into a minute, then eternity.

#

I work in my adobe studio under a grove of feathery mesquite trees atop a low red hill, ten miles north of Wickenburg. I gave the house a better roof and the Mare a new engine and transmission.

I don't know if I have the thirteenth orange. If the boy cheated himself, while the real magic sleeps above my worktable.

I stuck cloves into the orange, knotted it into a tether of silk ribbon. The scent is still strong enough to flavor the entire studio with lush night and wheeling stars. It astonishes visitors.

When I paint, one window looks south over the desert, to the mountains and mirages of Phoenix. The other gives me pure north light, and a view down a winding dirt road toward the highway to Nevada.

What Waits

1987

On such a day,
What waits beyond the mist?
New valleys, fresh roads,
Bridges flung over
Sparkling torrents that smell
Of rain and trackless miles of pine...
But this is the High Desert.
Nothing waits between
Mist and mountain
Save red rock,
Dry forests,
And the dream of water.

Place Codes

2014

85048
Dry mountain slope
Fringed by denim and diamonds,
Born from a fake name.
Banal enclave too smug
To fight the freeway that will poison it.

    87410
    Autumn cottonwoods
    Flame gold in the river valley
    Petrified forests and potsherds
    Guard a watershed's clay ramparts
    Loved, but left behind.

81427
Slick black rock combs
Aquamarine water into froth.
High above, a lone oak
Mocks the steel staircase:
'You will dissolve into this river,
Into this cold cauldron-chasm,
Before I do.'

    33480
    Pink coral walls
    Catch sunset,

Palm thatch crawls
With insects
Looking out after dark
On the glittering crowd:
All maskless.
Someone coughs.
Pink coral walls
Cannot hold back
The plague or the sea.

Iron, Water, Fire, Gold

2020

A cast-iron Japanese teacup,
Enameled black inside,
The purest water I might safely drink,
A gel candle flickering with gold leaf
In the shape of a clear gem, meant to float
In pools beside glittering parties
But here combined in solitude and silence
On a grey silk cloth
Beside a porcelain dish with one cube
Of the darkest chocolate I can find,
And a cordial-glass brimming agave spirit.

    Iron, water, fire, gold.

How did this private ritual arrive?
Mary Stewert's Merlin in his crystal cave.
Patricia McKillip's Morgon
Walking the paths of a mountain grave.
Selenite spearing
Titanic lances across hidden desert caverns
Below white-hot Sierra de Naica skies.
A chance find of wedding candles at an outlet store
My gaze caught as it always has
By sudden glitter.
Two cups my love and I discovered
To celebrate

A new home, twenty years back.

　　Fill the cup with water.

Set the candle floating,
Light with a jeweler's torch for a purer flame.
The clear gel melts a well around the wick.
The gold flakes transcribe
A covection torus:
Rising, falling in time with my breath.

　　Iron, water, fire, gold:

Endurance, resilience, passion, joy.
A ritual I can evoke by thought alone now
Always calming,
Always focusing,
Always marking great change, sorrow, or triumph.
I pray to no gods.
I ask for no answers
That I cannot find, myself,
As I eat the chocolate,
Drink the liquor,
Douse the flame,
And still the spinning gold.

Isidre's Eyes

2010

"Go or stay, you daydreaming wench!" Someone poked at Isidre's ribs. Someone else tugged at her worn satchel. Isidre froze on the gangplank of the rickety old mail-boat *Denerida's Banner.*

Ignoring the other refugees cursing and shoving behind her, she stared up at a rich merchant standing under the canopy of the upper-passage deck.

The vermilion-robed girl beside him laid one hand over his. He gasped and pulled his hand away instantly. Isidre couldn't see his skin. When the girl traced one fingertip along the wooden railing, a faint smoke-wisp lifted before the sea winds blew it away.

Isidre stalked up the gangplank to the lower-passage deck, keeping in full view of the merchant and the girl. A warm segmented weight pressed down on Isidre's collar-bones, under the ragged scarf around her neck and shoulders.

The girl on the upper deck smiled, twisting a carnelian-beaded dark braid around her forefinger. Gold-dust paint shimmered on her cheeks, forehead, and wrists.

Fire washed behind Isidre's eyes, blocking her vision, filling her thoughts with black pressure and hot fury. "Benetai," she hissed the girl's name, then breathed out deeply, heat hissing between her teeth. Those pristine brown braids could be ash in a second, the stone beads burnt white. Benetai's skull could so easily become a blackened lump, until it cracked apart in steam and sparks.

Isidre wasn't clumsy enough to make the railing smoke. She could melt gold dust into a molten, spitting ball on top of a slab of ice or the open palm of a trusting acolyte. A test she'd passed on her twentieth birthday, just eight days gone.

Now Isidre's hands felt hot.

Benetai mouthed silently, in the Temple language so ancient that few of the refugees knew it: *You are but the lamp.*

No, Isidre shaped the silent words precisely. *I am the Flame-given-Flesh. The Wriah looks through my eyes. Not yours.*

Benetai snarled. The merchant dared pull her away from the railing with his good hand.

Did Benetai mean to goad her? Isidre breathed in cool air. Her satchel shifted again, from someone's too-inquisitive touch. She stepped hard on someone's sandaled foot, heard a yelp, and felt her satchel settle back against her side.

She glanced back down the dock, where bright bronze glints and red plumes swayed above the back of the crowd. Wriah-Temple soldiers waited to catch her if she bolted from the mail-boat. They wouldn't dare hurt her. Nor would they ever let her get this close to the sea again. She could summon earth-fire faster than Benetai could blink.

But on an elderly ship, with grumbling passengers and crew hostage to Isidre's smallest mistake?

The warm weight on her shoulders pressed down, funneling more heat into her flesh.

Isidre thought, very clearly, of the *Banner* wreathed in flames. Of a panicked crowd, pushing and shoving until half of them drowned within a yard of the docks. She thought of a sea-wind fanning the flames into the dockside warehouses, filled with flour, oil, and pitch. Not difficult to imagine firestorms climbing back into the city, tier by tier, until they curled around the black-roofed Temple highest on the Wriah's volcanic slope.

Isidre thought of herself, smoke-stunned, sinking into the harbor's blue water. She played it up, too, imagining her heat-scorched eyes still open in accusation.

The weight lifted contritely from her shoulders and the phantom flames vanished from her sight.

Isidre's own carnelian-beaded braids were probably still in a garbage heap outside the east gate halfway across the city. Her red linen shift and fine red leather sandals swung on a clothesline in a Southside shabby alley, in exchange for the tattered rags she now wore.

The Temple soldiers had still found her in less than three hours.

Benetai, Isidre thought sourly. The next-youngest of the Temple Flame-witches. Benetai would summon fire on a ship made of kindling, just because she could.

Isidre pulled her bleached grey linen scarf up across her throat, fingers caressing the base-metal hinged collar that hugged her neck and shoulders. The crude jewelry was stamped with flames, touched with red paint, and sparked with cheap red glass beads.

Whores would have shunned it for more accurate copies, when they danced in red gauze and redder torchlight. Lower-city firecallers might have treasured it, an image of the Great Collar of the Wriah.

That collar was seven links of filigree platinum in swirling fiery shapes, joined together to form a crescent covering its bearer from mid-throat to just above her breasts. Each link set with a freeform ruby nugget shaped like a jet of bloody flame, each gem filled with living sparks.

When Isidre hadn't worn it in rituals, the Collar lay on a black lava plinth in the heart of the Temple. As far as she knew, an illusion of it lay there still, inviolate until the next chosen priestess touched it.

Then it would be base-metal again, and the real Collar a blazing signal around Isidre's neck.

Passengers, ignorant of their imminent death by fire, settled on chalk-marked narrow spaces on the deck. Sailors, singing Deneridan love-songs to the sea, hauled up the stone anchor and pushed away with strong staves. Sails bellying in a strong wind, the *Banner* lugged forward, eager for the sea.

From the railing, Benetai crooked a summoning finger.

Isidre turned, finding a way to the stern.

The mail-boat was not smoke darkened, hunger-honed Ankuaket City under a dozing volcano.

While daylight lingered, while Isidre stood in the open around harmless sailors and passengers, she was safe. Murder was the last of her pursuers' options. She was just another beggar fleeing from Ankuaket, now that the war with Denerida was over and the borders opened.

She had enough of her mother's hoarded money to survive a while in Denerida, if she could elude Benetai and the Temple assassin dressed like a merchant.

She glanced up at the survey deck again. Benetai had closed her eyes in trance. Isidre wished her the sea-gripe. The assassin wasn't looking at Isidre, but down to the deck toward

the first of the *Banner's* two masts.

A woman lounged by a hatch: a burly, strong-faced Deneridan with cropped blonde hair and olive skin. Isidre had seen her while scouting out the *Banner* before boarding it. Another of the crew?

No, Isidre thought. The woman had never been really busy, unlike the rest of the ship's people. The assassin looked as if he'd just swallowed a rancid cheese.

Another Temple lackey out to collect the bounty on Isidre? Or a Deneridan counter-agent? Isidre didn't know they were interested in her. She chuckled softly, settling back to enjoy the show.

The assassin looked back at Isidre. He gave her a harmless, ingratiating grin when he thought Benetai couldn't see.

Isidre kept her own face expressionless. Under her stolen shirt and scarf, the collar warmed, still dreaming of mayhem.

The Deneridan laid aside the net she toyed with, stood up easily on the rolling deck, and started toward Isidre.

The Temple assassin lost his mask just long enough to reveal a worried expression. Then he shrugged, grabbed Benetai's arm, and walked to the other end of the upper deck.

When Isidre lost sight of him, she turned to find the Deneridan woman gone as well.

#

The refugees weren't allowed to light their fire pots on deck. Isidre mingled with them, shared their grumbling as they paid for hot food from the galley. Two of her bronze coins bought a rubbery strip of cold fowl and a hunk of dark brown cane-sweetened bread.

Back in her paid-for spot on deck, she eyed the food sourly. Two more coins would have meant hot roasted chicken. She didn't have to be as miserly with magic as with her coins.

Isidre shut her eyes, feeling once again a heavy, rooted stillness, a seductive sense of being tied to the very earth by a slippery cord of invisible silk. Around her in the red-black void, she sensed magical traces of the sea. Glowing washes of blue radiance delineated the surface and deeper currents of the water. The people around her were glowing upright red blobs. Red-orange sparks of sea and air-life hurtled past, bobbing placidly with the motion of the sea, or darting under the waves.

The great flame-witches of legend would have reached out to that treasure house and plundered it, leaving dead husks drained of the life-fire.

Isidre merely turned her altered sight inward, to brush against the core of deep red radiance that flared within her.

She felt the spasm of trapped magic when, miles behind her now, the Wriah rumbled and stretched in its sleep. Even at this distance it knew her lightest touch.

How far away did she have to be before the collar lost its perverse personality? Before it turned into something that could be sold or safely destroyed? The city-state of Denerida was thirty leagues down the straights. It had been harassed for centuries by Ankuaket's magic, as had cities leagues beyond it.

Isidre hated to think of selling the collar. Even worse, the thought of being its guardian all her life. Someday she would find an apprentice to carry the collar in her place. And how then would she know the relic wouldn't be misused in some future time?

It had been waiting for a direct order, like a gazehound whining and tugging at the leash.

Eagerly, the collar stabilized the power flow up from within Isidre, allowing her stocky body and mortal nerves to channel waves of raw earth magic. They sang along her veins like a second heartbeat, strong enough to shake a city apart.

No, Isidre said silently. *Not that much power.* For a second, the collar grew just hot enough to make her skin uncomfortable. Isidre bore it with grim humor. The relic seemed to enjoy freedom as much as she did. The power cycled down to a bearable thunder in Isidre's bones.

Still blinded in her own trance, Isidre guided a small flicker of heat into the cold lump in her hands. It turned warm after a heartbeat. Rich, fatty odors of the cooked fowl and fresh bread seemed better than perfume. Isidre sighed, lifting herself out of trance, letting the collar absorb any leftover magical energy.

Before she could bite into the now steaming morsel, a woman's disbelieving voice said: "You. You roasted a chicken leg with the three-thousand-year-old Collar of Ankuaket? It took the Deneridan alliances fifty years to fight twenty-seven flame-witches and an army to a stalemate."

While it was still hot Isidre took a deliberate bite of her prize, chewed slowly, then swallowed. The chicken was delicious. She lowered the rest of it from her mouth. "Did they? I never heard an exact tally."

"How many people did you turn to ash on the front lines?"

The big blonde's contempt somehow stung Isidre more than any Temple whipping. "None. When I wore the Collar, I stayed in the temple. Didn't have a choice." Isidre lifted one trouser-hem, exposed the healed pink scar around her ankle. "They chained me to the altar. I told the generals that if they put me in the battle, I'd ash them first."

The blonde sat down beside her, in lanky crosslegged disarray. "And they didn't kill you? You are Isidre, aren't you?"

"I am. They can't. I have a friend who doesn't want me dead," said Isidre, offering a shred of the chicken.

"Well, that's settled," the Deneridan said, shaking her head. "I've already eaten. I'm Shvarna Eastinglas. Your new bodyguard. The Deneridan High Council wants very much to talk to you. They offer you your rightful place as a free noblewoman in return for information about Ankuaket's remaining defenses and its leaders. It's quite legal. Your father was a Deneridan war hero, after all."

"He was a scruffy spy Mother took a liking to and harbored for a month," Isidre said practically, "To the great disgust of several hopeful Ankuaket princes. They never could bring themselves to court me in earnest. I wasn't worth it. I'll repay them the favor by not betraying them," Isidre continued between bites of her dinner. "They're not worth it. I just want to get away from Ankuaket."

"We can talk about that after we neutralize your two trackers."

"We?" Isidre asked. "I have a bodyguard already."

"It's obvious that you can't or won't take care of them alone. You've done well this far, but you have to sleep sometime."

Isidre involuntarily raised a hand to her throat, but kept back her own acid comment. At least she'd got the Collar trained to warn her before it set fire to sneak-thieves. "You're probably right. The assassin and the witch will try for me tonight. Will you help me? I need a few things from the captain."

Shvarna grinned. All bravado in the face of uncanny witchery, Isidre decided. So fragile. So very human. She wanted equally to warm herself in Shvarna's blustering certainty, and push the woman away for safety.

No dalliances until she had dealt with Benetai and the collar was house-trained to behave away from its temple. At least the collar remembered liking Isidre's father.

Generals were all fools, no matter whose armies they commanded. Isidre wearily played out her arrival in Denerida. They wouldn't understand when she denied them.

While Shvarna was away talking to the captain, Isidre wove magic around her spot on the stern deck. Even on the crowded boat, other passengers suddenly felt a pressing need to be elsewhere.

By the eigth bell after noon, the western sky had almost lost its purple twilight afterglow. Sentries dozed. Refugees huddled together, dreaming of gentle hearth-fires and subtropical Deneridan sunshine.

The stars uncloaked themselves and wandered in slow arcs like the running lights of lost galleons. Watching them, Isidre felt almost carefree again. She would not leave the open horizon, after so long in a screened, incense-fogged temple.

She had tactical reasons, too.

An enclosed space might collapse from fire damage, or have all the air sucked out of it by a canny opponent's strike. Flame-witches had to have fuel, after all, the same as their weapons.

Isidre felt the collar warm gently against her throat as it reflected her emotions. For once, it wasn't roaring for battle. She felt its confusion. It had known only a simpler view of the universe, before her and her father.

This is freedom, Isidre thought. *Uncertainty is the price we pay for not being slaves.*

The collar's uneasiness focused tighter, on Isidre herself.

I'm not going to sell you or destroy you. No matter what. You're beginning to think about death. That means you can think about life, too. That you are alive. Life should be protected. Will you let me protect you?

The collar sensed someone walking quietly toward her. Warning heat from the hidden rubies made Isidre duck and roll away from her place by the railing. She'd been outlined against the starlit sea.

Shvarna let out a low whistle of surprise and approval. "Isidre?" she asked quietly. "I've got the damp fleeces you wanted. I didn't know you could move so fast."

"That might not have been you," Isidre muttered. The collar behaved oddly, still testing its surroundings as if it wasn't sure Shvarna was alone. "For all I knew, it was our fine gentleman from Ankuaket."

"Not him." Shvarna tossed a bale of water-sodden sheepskins at Isidre's feet. "He made the mistake of telling the captain you were a thief who'd stolen some jewelry from his daughter. I told the captain you were a Deneridan operative on official business. My credentials were higher. And the captain knows your father, apparently. Your assassin is currently being entertained at an officers' dinner."

"Detained, you mean. He was the civilized one," Isidre sighed. "Where is Benetai? The girl?"

"Back in her cabin, of course. Why? She's just a child."

Already ducking, Isidre heard Benetai's low, measured laugh, followed by a blast of breath-sucking heat and pressure.

The collar dropped its ugly disguise, the rubies flaring in a thermal shriek. Isidre rolled again, trusting the collar to shield her as she passed underneath the second blast.

Benetai had been clever. No visible fire to warn the sailors, just a cone of deeper blackness edged with faint, colorless flickers. Very little noise. Just a deep toned hum only a note or two different from the thrumming sails, as the *Banner* plowed leadenly through the waves.

Shvarna, with no other warning than Isidre's retreat, ducked a moment too late. One inadvertent gasp, soft as a sigh, told Isidre when the other woman made the mistake of breathing in Wriah fire. Shvarna staggered and fell.

Isidre scrambled behind the damp sheepskins and tossed most them over the unconscious Deneridan.

"I hated you for so many things," Benetai said. "For being the High Flame's bastard daughter. Always the one I had to match. 'Isa put her hand unscathed in fire when she was only four.' Or 'Isa turned down even the prince's offers, see how pure and holy she is!' When your mother jumped into the volcano after the peace treaty, the Collar chose you. Why?"

"She said it liked my father. It missed him after he got away."

"I told the generals you would steal it. Subvert it. Use it to destroy our Empire."

"I didn't steal it, I asked it to come with me," said Isidre, watching the faint light outlining Benetai's shape. "I ran away. Our Empire was a lie told by rich people stealing fire from the earth."

No flowing robes now or clinking charms now. The girl had actually thought a little, donning a dark grey tunic and trousers.

A competent adept, but not wise. The *Banner's* deck timbers smelled of hot pitch and scorched wood. Too much heat in too small an area. Isidre had another vision of the mail-boat wrapped in a sheet of flame.

She spared a little magic to keep the other passengers and crew asleep. It kept them out of her way. If she failed, they'd have a more merciful death.

The collar wanted to scorch the air from Benetai's lungs.

No, Isidre thought at the collar. *She's young enough to learn better.*

Benetai hit her with another wash of unseen fire. "Fight me," she growled.

"No," Isidre said aloud. The sheepskins sizzled. The smell was appalling. She drew in heat, keeping it from the railing, the deck, and Shvarna.

Benetai realized she merely fed the collar's power, and stopped. "Will you come back to your rightful place in Ankuaket?"

"No," said Isidre.

"Then give the collar to me," Benetai crooned, stalking from concealment and holding out her hands. Her thin body was edged in weak ripples of deep red light. Her eyes seemed inhumanly huge and dark. "You'll never use it properly. What can you do with Wriah fire? You who would rather be a beggar than the very Queen of Flames?"

"I'll be a free beggar."

"The Deneridans only court you because they want to explode the Wriah and destroy Ankuaket."

"I know. I'll deal with them," Isidre said.

"You'll not leave this ship alive unless you give the collar to me."

Isidre laughed and said, "Why? Anything you throw at me, the collar will block. Or eat."

"As long as it wants to obey you," Benetai said. "I am only five years behind you in training, Isidre. Did you think you were the only one destined to wear it? Does it miss raining fire? Heaving black, hot clouds of ash at enemy ships? Doesn't it remember the screams of sacrifices, the smell of burning flesh? It can have them again, if it chooses me."

The Collar remembered.

Isidre remembered the smell of roast chicken.

Benetai hummed.

Isidre stepped back. Benetai ignored Isidre completely, aiming her low, discordant song and agile thoughts straight at the collar. Isidre caught the trailing edges of the visions Benetai showed the relic: enemy and rebel ships on fire in a dozen harbors, Deneridan city walls melted into slag, the Wriah smoldering triumphantly over a Ankuaket restored to empire, rank smoke trailing up from a hundred altars like miniature volcanic plumes.

But none of it smelled like roast chicken did to Isidre's nose. Or felt as enjoyable as play-acting like a bit of beggar's jewelry.

I won't order you not to serve Benetai, she told the collar. *You know what tasks she will give you. You know what I would do. This is another price of freedom. Choose!*

Isidre lifted her hands to the elaborate catch at the nape of her neck, undid it, and tossed the glinting collar to an astonished Benetai. "Take it. I'm tired of your games, little girl."

Benetai smiled at the treasure spilling across her hands. The spun platinum filigree shone like frost under sea-glow and starlight.

Seven scarlet eyes woke within the ruby nuggets. Isidre thought they peered back at her.

"Mine," said Benetai hungrily, smoothing the collar around her own neck. It wouldn't stay latched shut, so she held it to her shoulders. She closed her eyes to enter a rapport with the relic.

And failed, opening her eyes in shock. "It won't do anything! Did you damage it, Isidre? If you've given me another fake, I'll kill you," she hissed.

"It's real. Try a specific command," Isidre said, gritting her teeth in apprehension. She thought she knew what command Benetai would give.

The young priestess pointed at Isidre. "Ash her in Wriah fire! Down to bone and beyond, and do not betray me to the guards with your light!"

Rubies burst into their full radiance, raking red gleams from nearby wood and metal. Isidre couldn't help from cringing. A beam of ruddy light lanced out toward Isidre, covered her from head to toe, brightened steadily until it was pale gold and warm as blood. The light faded, gentle as a caress.

Who among the flame-witches had seen their volcano from the inside?

Now two witches glimpsed dormant lava-tubes clogged with precious metal and jagged crystals, the deep, living arteries full of pulsing magma. Some of the molten stone forced its way out of the rock, trickling like syrupy rivers over the Wriah's flanks.

A mountain slowly learned to think.

Each river contained one branch of a fragmented intelligence, bumbling over the trails of its cooled and blinded predecessors. Old and earthbound, its power hedged by limitations of heat and pressure, its ceaseless quest outside the caldera always thwarted by cold air and the inevitable sea.

It kept looking for others of its kind, the dancing wave-forms moving through an ocean of molten rock far below.

Up in the cold atmosphere the fire rivers coiled around groves, puzzled and disappointed when the blooming trees caught fire.

As if from a thousand eyes, both Flames saw the tiny, wood walled settlement of ancient Ankuaket undergo the same scrutiny and the same fate dozens of times. People shouted, screamed, grabbed their most treasured possessions and raced for the little bundled-cane canoes that bobbed along the black sand beaches.

Over and over the people ran from rivers of living fire, until at last the frustrated spirit of the Wriah turned inward to harness its deepest magics.

Isidre and Benetai saw again what proud Ankuaket had long forgotten: the moment when a tribal shaman stubbed her toe on a barely cooled lava shoal, cursed the mountain with tired familiarity, and uncovered a glittering collar with seven ruby eyes.

"It's a live thing," whispered Benetai in shock, breaking the euphoric contact.

The collar clicked. The rubies turned incandescent against her skin, and their platinum settings pulsed with white fire.

Benetai screamed, clawing at the now-unyielding catch, as the collar turned its heat on her.

"No," Isidre told the collar. "Why not let her go, and come with me? If you are so hungry to see the world outside the mountain?"

The fires faded again. The collar dropped clinking on the deck. Isidre scooped it up, quickly fastened it around her own neck, and covered it with her stained and smelly scarf.

Benetai rubbed her collarbone and throat, where the skin was only reddened.

Isidre heard excited voices, feet pounding along the deck. So much for the sleep-spell. Benetai turned to run away, but Isidre caught her by the arm.

"It's a ship. Where would you go? Over the edge? You might yet convince the collar to live on your throat if you learn to behave. I won't live forever. It might get tired of me."

"You won't let it kill me?"

"I don't think it likes killing anymore." Isidre held the girl's arm tightly. "A lesson you should try."

"What's this?" blustered the captain, when he and his men reached the scene. "Someone yelled about a fire at the stern?"

"There was a fire, sir," said Isidre. "It is out now, and it will not start on your ship again."

Behind him, the 'merchant' from Ankuaket started to babble something about Benetai having been attacked by the refugee girl, but Isidre cut him off with an imperious cough.

She released Benetai and bent to uncover the still comatose Deneridan woman. "The Ankuaket priestess Benetai was experimenting with her magic. She accidentally hit Shvarna with a fire blast. By luck, I was unharmed. Shvarna breathed in some of the flames. She is not dead yet, though she needs help. Benetai is the only one here who can heal this woman fast enough. I will hold no grudge against her, if she does as I ask."

The captain nodded. "Seems fair," he said, eying Isidre's face as if he could see her father in her bones, then turned to the merchant. "See that your daughter makes her amends, or I'll let the Deneridan High Council know she brought Wriah fire onto my ship."

"But I can't heal!" Benetai wailed.

Isidre held out her hand. "Of course you can. Burn wounds should be the first thing a flame-witch learns to heal," she coaxed. "Give me your hand, so that I may lend you what little support I can give, priestess."

In a whisper, she went on: "Learn, Benetai. Make them think it's you doing this healing, and you'll save all our skins."

Benetai let Isidre bring their entwined hands around Shvarna's throat. Once again, the two were linked through the collar's network of fiery thought. A power that leveled mountains focused tighter and tighter. Comparing healthy flesh with scorched, coaxing new growth in a minute or less.

The onlookers saw only a few red glimmers and sparks that floated through the air and settled on the Deneridan woman, who began moaning and wheezing.

As soon as it was done, Benetai lunged away, eager to break Isidre's iron hold. Isidre ignored her.

"My nose itches," Shvarna coughed and turned on her side to face Isidre. "What happened? There was black fire. I breathed it. It hurt, but it's gone now."

"The young priestess had an accident," Isidre said. "That's all. She healed you in recompense. The itch is the dead skin still in your nose and throat. Liquid will help," she finished, commandeering a water-flagon from the grinning captain.

#

Before dawn, the *Banner* glided into a neutral fishing port to offload a few dozen refugees. The unlucky merchant from Ankuaket decided he had urgent business back in the city. His money would be missed, Isidre overheard from the chattering sailors, but not his arrogant daughter, who played with magics best left alone. She repeated this remark to Benetai, after catching up with the priestess on thedeck near the gangplank.

"So? Why should I care?" Benetai asked. Tears glittered in the younger woman's eyes. "What are you now, some gentle sheep that thinks I could be your friend? After you humiliated me in front of that rabble?"

"I'm not a sheep," laughed Isidre, shaking her short dark curls. "No one humiliated you. You're quite the little hero right now."

"No. You're the Deneridan hero's daughter," Benetai spat. "Will you run to him, now?"

"I don't even know him."

"I meant what I said, about the Deneridan plan for the Wriah," Benetai said. "We've known about it for years. You would have, too, if you hadn't been such a lonely misfit. You owe a debt to Ankuaket."

"The Deneridans will get the same reply I gave you last night: they can take the collar if they dare. If it likes them, then I'm free. If not, then I'm still protected and the collar simply will not do anything for them."

"But what of Ankuaket?" pressed Benetai. "You can't leave us without command of the mountain! What if Denerida decides to attack again, or some other army batters our gates? We'll have nothing but archers for defense."

"Ankuaket will have the same weapons any city has," said Isidre, stroking the warm collar under her clothes. "Arrows, spears, molten lead instead of molten stone, hot oil instead of hot ash and gas clouds. Have you ever thought of what we inadvertently taught the Wriah about people? Warfare. Hate. Destruction for its own sake. Forced sacrifice on the fire altars. You might try diplomacy and trade first."

Benetai cast her eyes down, hiding an emotion that Isidre hoped was shame, but rather doubted.

Spoiled from birth, resentful and afraid: Benetai might never completely shake off her indoctrination. Then again, the world might open her mind.

Isidre stepped backwards until her searching hand met the sleek solidity of the rail. "While Ankuaket commands those things, I cannot return."

"They'll send others after you," said Benetai. "Whether you're a beggar or a princess, the Flame Guards will follow you, waiting for a moment of weakness to take the collar."

"Tell them not to sneak around, then. Tell them to come honestly. I'll try to teach them, honestly. I'll give the collar to the first person it freely chooses."

"Dreamer," said Benetai. "Someone will trick you someday."

For a moment, Isidre felt lost and adrift in a memory of smoke and war. "They'll be trying to trick a living fire, whose wellsprings follow every volcano. Not very safe for them. I'll just stay clear of dead ground."

She looked out across the tiny bay to the blocky adobe buildings of the port, silhouetted in deep blue against the clear golden stain of a cloudless sunrise. Lamps glowed amber in many windows. Isidre heard young voices soar up in a spontaneous dawn song. Shvarna, still stubborn about her commission as a bodyguard, waited up at the Banner's bow, with a captain suddenly mindful of Isidre's every comfort.

A splash made her look down. The assassin glowered up at Benetai, from a long raft laden with debarking refugees.

"Will you go with him? Or stay with me?" Isidre asked.

"You'd teach me? After I tried to kill you?" Benetai seemed merely puzzled.

Isidre tried a language Benetai might grasp. "The collar did not kill you. How do you think the Wriah Temple elders will greet you, once that is known?"

"They'd kill me. Or cage me, to breed new Flames for the day they regain the collar." Benetai glowered down at the assassin, then looked at Isidre's neck. "Someone besides that surly Deneridan has to watch over you and the collar. Might as well be me."

"Good enough," said Isidre, feeling a single thread of watchfulness tangle between Benetai and the collar. The girl might not sense it for years. One life at a time, Isidre thought. "I'm hungry. Do you smell chicken?"

Handprint

2005

What came first, the hand or the brain?
We are not the only animal to use tools,
But perhaps the only one
To worship them
After forgetting how we made them.
We make fire, flint knives,
Cathedrals and microchips.
We weave myths and excuses,
Raise up gods
From crossroads and darkened mirrors.
We confuse art for reality,
Image for inspiration.
Extol the made,
But forget the makers:
Such is our handprint on the world.

Archivista, Part 1

1993

Beyond that city is the Lake of Rainbows.
Where the mountain stream feeds the lake
Waits a low house roofed in coral tiles.
Below the tiles there is a courtyard,
Beyond its open door,
A glimpse of diamond-stacked shelves
Holding ten thousand scrolls.
In the courtyard there is a fountain.
By the fountain stands a forge,
Coals glowing under noon-shaded pines.
By the forge stands a smith,
Her head cowled by white leather.
And under the leather,
Two eyes which lift,
And opening under black lashes, shine
Two half-moons of molten silver,
A hot silver voice follows after:
"I am the Archivista,
What would you have me make,
And what will you pay?"

Archivista, Part 2

2017

Into the blue halls of Festival,
Her mask of mildness askew over
Razor'd smile, slinks the Archivista
In search of strong drink:

    'Woe and damnation, for such as I to love
    A Paladin!

I am not skilled in healing
Broken soldiers.
He sleeps now, home and safe,
Distracted by shiny objects, new quests,
And brown-sugar bacon.
And I, longing to levy bitter words and bloodshed
From the guilty,
Must not, ere I dismay my
Tender-hearted love.

    Innkeep of the Aspect Cthonic!
    Bring me Inanna's barley ale
    Hathor's sweet beer,
    Golden meads of Asgardr,
    And a draught from the Morrigan's black cauldron
    Behind thee!

For payment I have a gem lost from

The Nauglamir, two silver pennies
Filched from an old woman gambling
Her last dice of the day,
And an ondine's green glass beads.'

Lina and the Bad Sandwich

2015

The 1970s replica pillow was orange and avocado felt, with three-dimensional felt flowers in a violent shade of magenta. Lina's turquoise silk hand-stitching perfectly matched the old magazine photo the client sent as a reference. Sadly, so did the other colors.

Lina blinked, refocusing on a bland white wall. Complementary-colored flowers still sizzled in her vision. "My eyes. I need a break. Agne!"

"What?" Agne emerged from a fabric storage closet, draped like a queen in scarlet silk velvet swatches slung over her usual pastel floral gauze dress.

Lina tried not to bask in the other woman's dark gaze, and failed. Lina then tried a sad-puppy look of her own. "Take over, will you? We need this for a photo shoot tomorrow, and the rest of the build team has gone home for the day. Can't wait for the night crew. They can't sew worth shit."

"And you think I can?" Lina's puppy-dog eyes were not working on Agne, as usual.

"I've seen that Unicorn Tapestry knockoff you managed last year."

"That was art. This is..." The look Agne gave the pillow was priceless.

Lina never, ever wanted that look turned on her. She scuttled for the workroom door.

Agne yelped: "Oh, my poor eyes. I'm a tetrachromat, you can't expose me to things this horrible!"

#

In the break room Vitaly looked down his considerable nose at the ragged remnants of the office party lunch buffet. "Ah, Lina, this is a travesty," he greeted her without looking away from the table.

Lina looked at the table. Among the wreckage, several of the white serving platters held pristine, untouched burdens. "I agree. Wonder where they got the food. It was better than Sub Magic, but not as good as that Jewish deli down on Calle del Sol."

Vitaly held a clear, plain glass bowl in his left hand, and meditatively tugged on his unkempt grey beard with his right hand. "The food was adequate fuel. I was unwise to ask you to bring my share to me in the warehouse, or I would have seen the danger earlier. Any whole leftovers are fake food. Do not touch them. They are bad." He nodded at one enticing portion of dark-pink peppered pastrami barely stuffed inside a glistening golden bun. "That sandwich is especially evil."

"You only say that because the pickle looks so real," said Lina, edging around Vitaly's plaid-shirted bulk.

"It does," he mourned. "I would not be in this existential wasteland if your Agne had not eaten all the real pickles. It is in my contract. There are to be pickles."

For the millionth time, she's not my Agne, Lina thought. "The film studio props department has asked us not to call it 'fake food'. We're supposed to be testing the, ah, verisimilitude alongside real deli items. Anyway, how can fake food be evil?"

"It smells of bad things." Vitaly wrinkled his nose. "Even from this far away. For the cameras, it is well. For the stomach, not so much. Look close but not too close. That sandwich catches light the wrong way. I wonder if the props department made it, or if San Clemente has infiltrated us again."

"San Clemente Special Effects is not our arch enemy, Vitaly!" Agne yelled from the sewing room. "We have a little rivalry on bidding for props and photo contracts, that's all. Don't you have stop-motion sets to shoot for that car commercial?"

"Done," said Vitaly. He splayed his fingers across the bottom of the bowl and balanced it upright.

Lina saw the faceted crystal finial jutting between Vitaly's fingers, and realized the bowl was an antique-looking cake protector. One of three that she'd seen gathering dust on one of the highest cabinets in the shop pantry. All nested on stacks of...yes, white porcelain platters that matched

the ones currently on the lunch table. This close, better light revealed how the platter rims were incised with green and gold Art Nouveau floral patterns interwoven with ornate black Cyrillic letters.

She reached for a clipboard jutting precariously near the edge of the table, then flipped over the grease-stained top sheet. "Did you get a shot of the sandwich trays when Berkeley Props left them? The guys provided an inventory so we can check off their better attempts."

"Yes," said Vitaly. "I have passed judgment upon the fake Philadelphia Steak, the fake French macarons, the fake milkshakes, and the fake Dagwood. But notice, there is no entry for a pastrami."

There wasn't.

"That sandwich does shimmer," Lina muttered, leaning a little closer to look. The glistening egg glaze on the bun seemed suddenly too slick. And it thickened just at the point where the light hit it, for a sudden extra, enticing shine...

"Ah, ah," Vitaly warned, grabbing Lina's shoulder and hauling her back, just as a clear shiny pseudopod shot out in her direction. The mass lost impetus seven inches out when it crossed over the platter border. The pseudopod fell with a wet plop to the serving platter and visibly flinched back from the border pattern.

Lina's face had been six inches away from the sandwich.

Vitaly calmly brought the cake protector down onto the platter. The crystal finial shone luminous ruby-red for a moment, and the same red fire ran along the rim between clear glass and white porcelain. Inside, the sandwich was abruptly not a sandwich, but a little heaving pile of glittering grey dust. Its particles were so fine it sloshed around like old-fashioned copier toner powder.

Lina hyperventilated: "Gah. That...that is not a sandwich."

"Do not worry, Lina. It cannot escape for another seventy-three minutes. My grandmother's china is very sturdy."

"Seventy-three...oh gods above, tell me that isn't what I think it is?"

Agne hugged her from behind. The taller woman's warm touch felt like an anchor in a grey maelstrom. "Easy, princess," said Agne. "We've got this."

Vitaly rumbled, "Seventy-two minutes. I have long suspected the props department of San Clemente to be in league with minor demons, but I suspect they have outdone themselves this time. It is now very illegal to open portals to any world infected by this...what do you call it in English? Grey Goo?"

"Call the cops," Lina wheezed.

"I have done so already," said Vitaly with a dark grin quirking his mustache. "San Clemente must have found a way to cut corners by convincing the Goo to shapeshift on command. But they would not have the proper spellwork to guide and contain it for long. I know this, because they did not retain my services when they had the chance."

Behind Lina, Agne gave an eloquently scornful snort. Lina felt more of her brain cells start to come back online from the abyss of sudden fear.

"Vitaly, who exactly opened the portal at San Clemente, so they could even summon this Goo?"

He gave Lina an innocent look. "You know I do not violate the terms of their restraining order. I have not been present near their facilities for ten years. It is true, that I may have left some spellbooks behind, inadequately concealed in their reference library."

Agne heaved a great sigh. "And just as possible those spells were deliberately written awry?"

"Hmph. A basic understanding of thaumaturgy would reveal the flaws. I cannot be responsible...sixty-seven minutes...for the actions of idiots who think they know more than they do. It is, how is the phrase? The Dunning Kruger Effect?"

"Well, now it's our problem. The Corps will be just as likely to annihilate our studio on the grounds of contamination," said Lina.

"I am thinking dragonfire could do the job before law enforcement arrives?" Vitaly offered in as small a voice as he had.

"Let me guess, you didn't exactly report it as Goo?" Agne laid her forehead on Lina's right shoulder. For a moment, the other woman's jasmine and citrus perfume sizzled across Lina's brain.

"I did not. Only as a 'suspicious lifeform'. Sixty-five minutes." The big man carefully scooped up platter and cake protector, leaning close to watch the grey mass within batter at the crystal dome with steely claws. They didn't leave a mark.

"Vitaly, I get it. You are one vengeful and powerful lizard, and those pricks at San Clemente probably had it coming. But did you stop to think about the innocent people you might have endangered?" Lina tried to keep 'friend' in her voice, and 'schoolteacher' out. A lecture wouldn't help.

"If I had thought they would do more than summon minor demons, I would never have left those grimoires. To reach out to The Worlds Without Magic? To summon an Eater-of-Worlds? Only idiots would do that and think they could win."

"Only idiots could think that dragonfire would not leave the tiniest speck of Goo for the inspectors to find," said Lina.

"One dragon, maybe. Two, working together, and one of those far older and stronger than myself? Having my grandmother's china here was lucky forethought on my part, but it will not solve the problem. Fifty-eight minutes. Agne?"

Lina felt Agne's hand clench on her other shoulder. Not lifting her head, Agne asked, "How long have you known, Vitaly?"

He shrugged, keeping the tray utterly level. Inside the dome, the grey powder splattered against the crystal with barely audible pings. "Since the day Master Ermundsen hired you. You did not seem eager to reveal it. I thought it a matter between you and him."

"Wait," said Lina, catching up to the really important stuff that the Goo had interrupted. "Agne. You're a dragon? What, is everyone here nonhuman but me?"

She was treated to Agne's warm, soft exhale on her upper back, and the other woman's low giggle. "No. But you are my princess, just so you know."

"Fifty-six minutes, Agne," Vitaly warned. The pings had changed sound, a little deeper and more resonant.

Agne finally lifted her head and made a hmmming noise of consideration. "The back parking lot?"

Lina felt a budgetary headache coming on. "Ermundsen just got it repaved from the unicorn rampage after that cowboy flick."

"Then he can get it paved again. We can't flame until we shapeshift, and we can't shift inside here, much less flame. We're lucky we're on a slow day, and everyone else gone until later," said Agne.

She slid her strong bronze-gold hand down Lina's shoulder, arm, and clasped Lina's fingers loosely in her own. One gold and blue-opal ring glowed against Lina's lighter skin. "Princess? We'll take care of this, then do dinner? There's a new Indian fusion café I really want to try, if you can handle hot and spicy?"

Lina let herself be tugged along, thinking *dragon*, and *Agne*, and *Princess*. Sneaky lizards.

#

Towering salt-cedar trees shielded the parking lot from street views on the sides where tall, blank warehouse walls didn't. Lina knew Ermundsen had set powerful don't-notice-us wards around the building, as well.

She watched Vitaly walk to the center of the asphalt-paved lot and set down the cake platter.

Agne muttered something and went back inside the warehouse, returning with the favorite coat that she kept, winter and summer, hanging on her workshop wall. Based off some full-skirted Tibetan design, it featured embroidered and beaded panels in rich jewel-toned fabrics.

Dragons were embroidered on many of them, Lina noticed.

"You need to wear this, Lina," Agne ordered, bundling Lina into the coat.

Moving faster, Vitaly joined Lina in the shadow of the shipping-bay doorway. "Ah, a spellcoat. Good idea, it will keep her warm," Vitaly said as he swept off the top layer of a stack of cardboard to reveal a clean surface. He began shrugging out of his plaid flannel shirt.

Agne's coat held traces of her perfume and body scent. If not for the Goo, Lina might have been swooning just a little.

"Hey!" Lina yelped when it became obvious Vitaly would not be stopping with underwear. She turned around to see Agne doing the same thing. Humor and resignation battled on Agne's face.

Lina felt herself flush red with embarrassment from ears to neck, and turned to face the stack of cardboard instead. On one half, Vitaly's dull-toned garments piled up in a heap. On the other were Agne's neatly folded dress, pink cotton undies, and all her jewelry.

"Magic is magic and science is science," Agne chuckled from entirely too near Lina's shoulder. 'You have never seen a shapeshifter move from a small-mass body to a larger mass? There are certain protocols we must follow."

"And you, little one, you should stay back here behind Ermundsen's secondary wards," Vitaly said, as his quite naked self stalked back out to the lot.

"Eh, if we fail, it's not like she'll have time to be afraid," said Agne, patting Lina's shoulder.

Lina risked a glimpse of her two now-naked coworkers facing each other over the cake platter.

She looked aside, feeling the wrongness of the moment. The first time she saw Agne nude, it should be private and near-sacred.

Upon self examination, Lina thought the dragon development didn't change how she felt at all.

"Lina, look away if you haven't, already. There will be a bright flash," Agne warned.

Lina had closed her eyes, but the flash lit up her vision blood-red anyway. The air crackled with cold. When it subsided and Lina dared to look, the ice-frosted parking lot was overwhelmed with dragons.

Since the multiverse barriers had been breached, magical folk were more common, but dragons of any type were still a rarity. Or, Lina realized, they just stayed in human form most of the time.

That oil-black glittering creature with the wise-looking tentacle beard and stocky body had to be Vitaly. That left Agne...

Oh. Agne.

Agne was twice as massive as Vitaly, her long lean body shaded from midnight blue along her spine and delicate-looking head to silvery salmon-pink on her belly. Her unfolded blue wings rose as high as the salt-cedars, casting deep shadows around the cake tray.

The cake platter pulsed vivid scarlet at twenty-second intervals.

"Lina, look aside," Agne called in a voice like silver thunder. The two dragons backed away from the cake platter until their hindquarters met warehouse walls.

Lina obeyed, seeing orange light brighten to blue-white on the inside wall, her own shadow seeming cut from a black abyss. Tucked in Agne's coat, she felt ridiculously safe.

The roaring blast-furnace of dragon fire went on so long the air went from deeply-cold to hot, ripples of heat making Lina's shadow waver on the wall. The coat helped with the heat, too.

She wondered if the dragons could destroy all the Grey Goo, and whether she'd have any warning if they didn't.

The roar stopped so completely Lina still heard it in her mind. Instinct or the coat made her keep turned away from the parking lot, as a second blast of heat rushed by.

"It is possible that we have succeeded," Vitaly called in a normal human voice.

"But you should maybe wait until we're decent?" Agne said, laughter and relief behind her words.

#

Two hours later Ermundsen and the Supernatural Enforcement Corps police found all three of them sitting on the battered wood benches flanking the back parking lot.

The coat was back in Agne's workshop. Lina lounged across Agne's lap, having her hair braided with tiny golden bells shimmering with magical wards even in Lina's peripheral vision. She and Agne shared a bottle of root beer. Vitaly had something black, alcoholic, and fuming white. A safe distance away a twenty-foot-wide, ten-foot deep crater of black glass crackled as it cooled.

"That's from dragonfire," said one of the Corpsmen in an impressed tone.

"My undercover security detail," said Ermundsen, unruffled as always in his neat black suit. "One of them is always on duty just in case. They're very effective. Still, we should make certain there's no trace of banned lifeforms in the crater."

The Corps team moved away from the crater's perimeter after fifteen minutes of surveying. Their senior officer shook her head. "Not here, and not inside the premises. Better a false alarm than having to ash a city block, Master Ermundsen. Master Ostrovky, you mentioned a prop pastrami sandwich wasn't on the contractors' list. Do you have any idea where it might have been introduced into the shipment?"

Vitaly opened his mouth, but Agne was quicker. "You should look at a trade show production company called San Clemente Special Effects, across town. They have…a history of industrial espionage and magical accidents. Master Ostrovsky can vouch under oath he was let go from San Clemente for whistleblowing a decade ago." She had a much better innocent-voice than Vitaly.

"I can verify that," said Ermundsen, and Lina could almost have kissed him.

#

"Right," said Ermundsen once the Corps had left, with promises to give him money to repair the parking lot. "Since I now have two dragons on my security staff, could you explain just what in the hell was going on?"

"The prop folks were setting up a display, and I thought it would be classy to use Vitaly's old cake platters," said Agne.

"I thought the pastrami looked evil when I saw it later. It was grey in too many places, and too shiny in others," said Vitaly. "We are lucky it was magically restrained while the rest of the staff were eating lunch around it."

"We are lucky you happen to have magical cake platters made for Russian royalty, you mean," said Ermundsen.

Lina had a litany of supportive not-quite-lies ready to go, when what actually came out of her mouth was, "I'm dating Agne!"

"It's about damn time," said Ermundsen. He loosened his tie, snagged another bottle of the smoking beer from Vitaly, and thunked down on the bench beside him.

After a swig of the black stuff, he gave them The Look.

"It was Grey Goo," Agne said sheepishly

"It tried to eat my face," said Lina.

"I didn't think they'd use my doctored journals to summon that," said Vitaly.

Ermundsen let a small grin preempt his unassumingly-bland businessman face. "I believe someone had to give them the idea, first. To be fair, I had no idea they'd try summoning a banned lifeform from across the Barriers. Here's to San Clemente and industrial espionage. It goes both ways, suckers," he intoned, holding up the bottle in toast. The others joined him after a moment.

Safe in Agne's arms, Lina had an awful thought and just as promptly voiced it. "What else did you leave in those journals, Vitaly?"

I Have Stolen Them (Or, Why Fanfic)

2003

Yes, I have stolen them!
But no more honor has a jeweler for a gem,
Than I for these lovely gentlefolk
Yet like gems prized from battered crown
Or corroded ring and set again, more...
Or less...tinselly glittering,
They beg new voices to frame or refine
Such traits their true authors might decline
To set free in exploration: whole treasuries
Of joy, glory, grief, desire.
Some years I've spent inside created minds
While my own tale-spinning, lax, unwinds.
Is this obsession or apprenticeship?
They have stolen *me*,
These earthbound angels, these spirits of fire.

Arachne

2011

We work from the center of a web.
Every moment, strands shiver to the
Ticking clock,

    The passage of leviathans

Half-seen, slow voices counting
One number a year,
Always faster than glory
Inching from our fingers.

    Wind blows.

All our spinning
Frays to grey rags in the dusk.

    We do not own the web or the wood,

The steel or the silk.
But we own Vision
Until the moment we make it real.
Is this how Arachne felt?

    Not hubris, but love of the work

Challenged Athena,
A goddess

Only playing at her loom.
Milton dared us to reach for heaven.
Gods lay shadows on the path.

They cannot quench

The furious thunder within us.
Are they jealous?

The clock chimes:

Thread a new needle under starlight.

Copper Bells

2010

Davis and Worth talked at an isolated table on the hotel veranda, their faces and gesturing hands lit by a cut-glass candle lamp. From behind a potted palm tree, Eric Van Reiss eavesdropped on the two sorcerers.

"Kincaid lied," Davis said, bracketing the ornate lamp's chimney with his big hands. His

light-colored eyes narrowed in a perpetual sun-squint. Even from twenty feet away Van Reiss saw splashes of orange ochre and turquoise pigment ingrained along the famed artist's creased knuckles. "The Hopi and the Navajo tell no legends of rich tombs hidden in the Grand Canyon, nor did any of the Spanish padres who first mapped the area."

"Kincaid saw something." Worth's soft chin set in a stubborn angle. "The details he wrote!"

Davis grinned. "You know how these yellow journalists are, touting one sensational lie after another."

"Should I resent that remark?"

"Do you feel it was aimed at you, or Kincaid?"

As they bickered amiably, daylight faded west of the mountains. Blue dusk and white glass lamps revealed the manicured grounds and palm groves of Castle Hot Springs, Arizona's de facto shadow capitol. The Volstead Act had been repealed only a year before, so the booze was top-shelf, plentiful, and legal. With enough magic or money, the fortunate few might forget the desperate world outside this secret desert valley. Most of the current guests seemed to be inside the ballroom, listening to a piano concert.

Worth stared out into the twilight, his dark gaze sweeping by Van Reiss's hiding spot. "Kincaid vanished over two decades ago, in '09 right after that newspaper article. Bought off? Dead? Or worse? I enjoy puzzles that aren't mine, but this one troubles me." He slapped the table with both hands. His left wrist clanked on the wood.

Jostled, the candle flared up. Davis pulled back scorched fingers. "Mind the table, you little warlock. I don't want flaming wax in my lap."

Worth gave a twisted half-smile. "You can't believe that was just the wind, old man? Kincaid's 'hidden city under the high desert' could be far more than a tomb. Remember the Hopi legends of an underworld?"

"Their First World? Lost, they say. A paradise turned to dust and stone."

Worth nodded. "Just so. Ever hear of the translator Layard and the Sumerian death-goddess Ereshkigal?"

"No. Do they walk into a bar together?"

"Very droll. Layard deciphered the clay tablets from the ruins of Ur. Ereshkigal ruled a kingdom under the earth, the 'Houses of Dust' where the fading ghosts of humanity dwelled. Parallels to Hopi myth."

Davis scowled. "You're sending a common grave robber into a dusty house?"

Behind the palm tree, Van Reiss bit back a curse. He preferred the term 'adventurer.'

"Our lad Eric is anything but common."

"You should see the royalty skulking in Taos. Kings and countesses, poor as the rest of us after the Great War and the Crash." Davis waved insultingly at the lush resort beyond the veranda. "Pardon me, poor as some of us. How much did you bank last year off your last novel? Off your newspaper writing?"

"I'm still a commoner. The man who holds the key must be of regal lineage. That's how these old spells work."

Van Reiss grinned in the cool dusk. His father had died destitute in a drought-blasted Texas town, the family Bible the only gilt-edged relic of ancient wealth. Van Reiss lost the thing in a card game after the funeral. But he'd remembered the royal names within.

"There's more in northeast Arizona than dust," said Worth, his voice lowering. "How much gold and silver has been taken out of this land since the Spaniards swept through? Isn't it strange, how the pueblo-dwellers only used metal in copper bells and ornaments traded up from Mexico? When they lived atop some of the greatest metal deposits in the world? Material value aside, the art and artifacts in such a ruin would be priceless."

Van Reiss would rather just have the gold. Grifting and ruin-robbing earned scarcely enough cash for survival. He saw his future in every broken automobile alongside the western highways, and in every soup-line and migrants' camp.

#

Augustin Worth had found Van Reiss three weeks before, as the latter worked the nighttime edges of a pompous spring festival down in Phoenix.

What should have been an easy swipe from a fussy-looking businessman, turned into a honed knife in front of Van Reiss's face. The edge glinted with golden flickers of neatly-controlled magic as the smaller sorcerer pushed Van Reiss hard against an alley wall.

"Pickpocket?" said the man, and then: "Eric Van Reiss? I've been looking for you for a job."

Talk led to drinks in a gin joint in the basement of a swank downtown hotel. Worth laid down an envelope of cash and arranged for a new suit that Van Reiss could rarely have afforded on his own. Then Worth gave Van Reiss orders to do research, like some moon-eyed college boy running errands. The suit was worth some dusty hours in newspaper archives and college libraries.

#

Beyond the new Gershwin score playing in the resort ballroom, Van Reiss caught the silken growl of some social pinnacle's Packard protesting the rugged forty-mile trek from civilization. The breeze shifted again, playing with his hair, bringing a fetid breath of sulfur from the nearest hot spring pool.

On the veranda, Worth hissed: "Think, man! Kincaid's lost city could be real. The woman was, along with her plight."

Davis gave an outraged, full-body twitch. His hand nearly knocked over his glass. "Then let her stew in it! She's no doubt stuck there for a reason. The Navajo call the makers of such places the Anasazi, the Ancient Enemies. The Hopi are even less complimentary."

Worth leaned forward over the table. "Marshall Davis, try being a hero for once. How is life as an underpaid WPA artist? Do Valerie and the children like the hot spring pools and your bungalow? Is everything here at Castle Springs as fine as Dodge-Lujan's place in Taos, where you painted so many pictures last year? Pictures with no buyers?"

"You're no Grail Knight, yourself," hissed Davis, standing up.

"I found us a hero."

"The boy? Good luck with that."

Worth barked another humorless laugh. "Sit down, man. I merely point out the obvious. Yes, there's a pretty lady to restore to the light of day. But there are also human forces waking in Germany and Italy which could shatter our already-wounded world. If the Dwellers-in-Dust climb out to play now, selling magical paintings will be the least of your worries."

"You really want to search for this Cibola?" asked Davis, settling back in his chair.

"Me?" Worth chuckled. "No. I'm much more practical. I'm sending in the grave robber."

#

Van Reiss eased away from the palm tree, silently walking on grass beside the noisy crushed-stone path. There could be gold, but also a skirt in some kind of trouble. Depending on the trouble, this might be fun. Get the gold, get the woman, get away clean. He already knew ways to confound even Worth's magic. Instead of Mexico or California, Van Reiss revised his travel plans upward: the South Pacific, China, perhaps Australia.

Thirty feet out, he smelled more sulfur in the breeze, then the sweet corruption of dead flesh and rotting fruit.

A dark bulky shape eclipsed the lamps to his right. He'd marked it on the way in, a tall garbage canister on wheels, left out behind the kitchens near the isolated back veranda. The source of the foul smells, no doubt. As he looked, two dull, pale gleams ignited near the canister top.

The breeze blew dust in his eyes. Staggering back on the damp grass, Van Reiss lurched against the canister. He expected the contact to ring loudly, and led with his right palm first to muffle the noise. Not cold metal, but warm gritty stone met his flesh. His right shoulder hit a surface that yielded, softly grating under his weight. Hard, strong fingers gripped his left shoulder, drawing him into an embrace heavy as a wrestler's.

"Flee, little prince," a male voice rumbled in his ear. "Or join all Their lackeys in the halls of dust."

Wind thrashed the palms and cottonwoods, scattering torn leaves across the lawn. From the veranda, Van Reiss heard Davis cry out, then the wind's howl drowned all. Choking, Van Reiss pushed hard against the heavy grip, fighting free. The wind died swiftly, leaving the faint dank smell of vegetable rot.

He faced a steel garbage canister with two jutting screws near the top of its lid, points gathering light in a mockery of eyes. He brushed his clothes straight, and moved silently into cleaner air. Thirty more feet down the path, he stepped noisily onto the gravel.

#

Worth looked up at his crunching approach, and nudged an empty chair out from the table. "Van Reiss! Did you get the map of Kincaid's Grand Canyon expedition?"

"There is no map. Whatever Kincaid found, it's in Marble Canyon, not the Grand Canyon itself," said Van Reiss, sinking just to the seat-edge of the rawhide chair. Even before he'd settled, a waiter brought a third glass and another pitcher of tea spiked generously with whiskey.

"Kind of you to show, young man," said Davis, when the waiter retreated into the resort's main building.

Van Reiss tapped an overstuffed Manila envelope under his arm. "A mimeograph of Kincaid's Phoenix Gazette article from 1909. One of the Interior Department's maps of the area from two years ago. That's all I could get."

"Do you have a solid location on the map?" asked Worth, reaching for the envelope with his left hand.

Van Reiss let him have it, and tried to get a closer look at Worth's bronze bracelet. On its rough sand-cast surface, raised lines hinted at some kind of winged serpent. Then Worth shoved it once more under his cuff.

"I can guess to within a half-mile span of clifftop," said Van Reiss. "There are only a few places where Kincaid's tomb could be, nearly fifteen hundred feet straight down from the rim of Marble Canyon. Your Smithsonian contact in Phoenix won't guide us. He said the cave was sealed up before the War. No way in. No way to spot it from the cliff above, or from the opposite canyon wall. He wouldn't even pinpoint it on the map." The grifter's equation of risk and gain made Van Reiss probe: "He sounded scared. I went back to ask him more questions yesterday. His office was cleared out to the last paper. No forwarding address, when he'd paid rent for three more months."

Davis leaned back from the table, flexing his big knuckles in a way Van Reiss knew from prizefighters back East. "Spooked? Or greedy? Do we need to expect more treasure hunters?"

Worth shook his head. "He wouldn't talk to them. It was my name alone that got Eric through the door. The man's pension is at stake if any inquiries come back to the museum. No, there's something in that canyon. Kincaid spoke of fresh air circulating in the tomb. There will easier passages than the cliff entrance. I have what may prove a key." He turned toward Davis. "You brought your sketch of the Bell Dancer?"

The artist frowned, then lifted a battered black leather portfolio from under the table. He freed a single leaf of thick, textured watercolor paper. With just his fingernails, he shoved it across the rough-hewn wood. "Take it," he said. "I don't ever want to see her again."

Worth grinned. "Caused you problems with Valerie, did she?"

Van Reiss barely registered Davis's muttered answer.

The woman in the charcoal sketch had a rounded face with lustrous dark eyes, wide lips, flawless skin, and matte black plaits gathered into butterfly-wing shapes at each side of her head. Davis had drawn her with metallic bells clumping like berries in those braids, and hanging in pendant-rows from her heavy beaded necklace. White folds of finely-woven cotton, bordered with dark geometric patterns, wrapped her upper body but did not conceal the lines of her full breasts and narrow waist.

As if from far away, Van Reiss heard chiming bells, then a single plaintive flute.

The only colors on the sketch were touches of blue-green chalk on the woman's beads and coppery orange on her bells.

"Van Reiss. Eric," said Worth loudly, turning up the wick in the crystal lamp. "Look at the bloody bells, not the woman."

Van Reiss blinked in the stronger light and peered down. "Lotus flowers?" He leaned closer, focused through suddenly itchy, dusty eyes. Each tiny bell, similar to a European sleigh-bell in its rounded shape, was capped by the familiar petal-spiked cone of the Egyptian lotus. Davis had even succeeded in portraying chips of turquoise and malachite inlay in the petals, vivid against the copper.

Worth eyed Davis with wary respect. "You were far too close if you saw that much."

The artist nodded. "We were invited to a spring dance at one of the pueblos. No photographs allowed, which put Valerie into a snit, but the elders trusted me enough to let me sketch. This one," he tapped the edge of the paper. "She leaned on an adobe wall just inside the circle of torchlight, watching everyone else. I thought she waited her turn to dance, so I felt free to sketch her."

Van Reiss could not look away from the girl's gently-curved lips. He'd expected demure shyness or its mask. But Davis had drawn hints of an ironic smile.

Davis looked sideways at the drawing, as if a direct glance might hurt it—or him. "After I finished drawing, I realized no one else could see her. She walked right up beside me, told me she was a captive, and how to free her. She said in exchange for her willing portrait, I had to help her. I thought she was a stranded ghost."

Van Reiss sneered and said, "Ghost? With a smile like razors dripping honey? That's a real flesh-and-blood dame, old man."

Worth's other hand crept up to stroke the bracelet under his shirt cuff. "Oh, she's very real. A goddess. A New World Persephone. Or Layard's Ereshkigal."

"Worth," growled Davis. "Do not jest about the Bell Dancer."

"I'm not," said Worth, and threw down a waxed brown-paper package. It struck the table with a muffled jingle. He opened the parcel without touching the contents, and shook them out into the lamplight. A knot of dull copper shapes resolved into a copper tube, intricately-chased, a quarter-inch wide and only a little longer. From it fell a copper chain, its links folded into interwoven loops. On the chain swung three copper bells, their lotus caps inlaid with turquoise and malachite.

The very bells Davis had drawn.

"Where?" asked the artist, his worn face gone sallow under its tan.

"Some years ago I was walking up near Bitter Springs. These swung from a juniper twig directly in my path," said Worth.

Something in his crooked half-smile screamed 'liar, liar' to Van Reiss.

When Van Reiss' hand crept out to caress the bells, neither Davis nor Worth stopped him. The bells chimed as Van Reiss moved them back and forth across the table. He lifted them, wondering if they'd hung from the woman's hair or necklaces.

A flash of pain struck his fingers. He cursed and dropped the bells. Lamplight flickered again. Whiffs of mingled sulfur and jasmine stung his nostrils.

Davis groaned.

"Sharp!" said Van Reiss, squeezing his forefinger where one copper flange had nicked his skin. A drop of bright red blood welled up. He sucked it away.

"The resort has a doctor," said Worth.

Van Reiss laughed. "For this? It's already stopped bleeding. Badly wrought. No wonder she threw them away. Who is she, part of a caretaker family?"

"Of a sort. But she may be amenable to persuasion and a promise of a better life. The bells could be a key. Other explorers have mentioned odd caves and petroglyphs up on the plateau east of Marble Canyon, things they are never able to find again. We'll seek our door and our treasure up there."

The three men consulted other maps, drew up contracts and signed them.

They drank fortified tea late into the night, planning the supplies and vehicles necessary to conduct three men up into the wind-carved plains and deep defiles of the Colorado Plateau.

An hour before dawn, Van Reiss slipped into Worth's unlocked bungalow. Faint amethyst light from the window showed the envelope on a bedside stand. Davis's sketch and the packet of bells lay atop the envelope.

Worth snored a little as Van Reiss gathered the items. Van Reiss paused until Worth's breathing calmed to a slow, deep cadence. The man wore long sleeves even to bed.

His fingertips tingling, his own breath dry and metallic in his throat, Van Reiss could barely contain his excitement as he crept from the bungalow.

The garbage canister remained a lifeless box of sheet metal. If any sulfur stained the dawn air, the reek was buried under the perfumes of orange-flower, jasmine, and damp grass.

#

Van Reiss drove all day in his old Ford, reaching the trading post and modern inn at Cameron on the Little Colorado River near sunset. He took a room facing southwest, overlooking a winter-browned garden sheltered by high red sandstone walls.

In the late sunlight, the night's terrors seemed unreal. Worth had probably started those delusions in that bar in Phoenix, intentionally, with his wild tales of Kincaid and other explorers.

Van Reiss ate chili stew and buttered cornbread at the little café. The food seemed mushy and tasteless, though he saw other customers attacking it with gusto.

Alone in his room, he pulled out a cheap bronze chain from under his shirt. The sniffer talisman pendants still seemed inert. Shaped like a mermaid and a leaping greyhound, the two little tin whistles should spark at magical danger, or blow faint warning calls. They'd cost him a small fortune in Miami years ago, and had been faithful up to two weeks ago.

How much of a sorcerer was Worth? How much of his wealth came from his novels and

journalism, and how much from magic?

Van Reiss took the rest of his treasures to bed with him, arranging Kincaid's notes, Davis's sketch, and the waxed packet on the other half of the bed. The headline of the old article taunted him:

#

'Egyptian Artifacts in the Grand Canyon!
The Phoenix Gazette - April 5, 1909:
Remarkable Finds Indicate Ancient People Migrated From The Middle-East!
The latest news of the progress of the explorations of what is now regarded by scientists as not only the oldest archaeological discovery in the United States, but one of the most valuable in the world...'

#

Van Reiss, skilled at recognizing other con-men, thought the whole affair was bunko meant to sell newspapers.
After one vague and vainglorious article, Kincaid and his associates vanished. The Smithsonian disavowed all stories of the find. Dozens of caves opened out from the bone-pale cliffs of Marble Canyon, but none of their ruins held any hint of the Far East or Egypt. Even the recent expedition by Bernheimer and Wetherill, to document the famous Rainbow Bridge and Glen Canyon, had seen no trace of any ancient settlement more advanced than the Pueblo-dwellers' ancestors.
Before turning down the lamp, Van Reiss couldn't resist looking again at the woman in Davis's sketch.
He dreamed first of the blue horizon to the northwest: the Canyons of the Greater Colorado, where every horizon was sixty miles away. He'd never seen them in the waking world.
Then Van Reiss was somehow back down in Phoenix, among cool sleek rooms laden with expensive suits, the staff respectful of Worth's money.

The fitting girl brushed his new lapels flat against his shoulder, then tugged at his left cuff.

"There's a loose seam where the fabric gaps."

She didn't call him 'sir', she looked him boldly in the eye instead of smiling demurely when he patted her shapely rear, and she turned and planted a damned straight pin right into his inner right forearm.

"Hey!" Van Reiss yelped. He remembered this happening, but the girl had been a blonde, not a bronze-skinned enchantress.

"A little sting to wake you up, my king," she mocked, then thawed into an unnerving sympathy. "Turn around. Run away. Don't follow the bells."

He forgot her words three breaths after waking before sunrise.

#

Under an empty blue sky, he followed the highway north, at times near-frantic to dodge around more tourists in their slow vehicles. Whirlwinds paced him on the right or left, sometimes near, sometimes half a mile off.

An inner whisper coaxed him to turn the Ford left onto a shepherd's or surveyor's track. Twin ruts cut red scars between pale golden grasses and lavender-green sagebrush.

Van Reiss drove west until the Ford's wheels lost grip in the deep ruts. He saw a buzzard idly riding spring thermals a mile west over the canyon.

He grabbed the envelope, then dropped it. His cut finger was greyish white as marble, tiny scrapes standing out in red streaks. Van Reiss grabbed the envelope with his other hand.

Two more dust-devils twisted on either side of him, not fifty feet away, thin skeins of pink against the turquoise sky. They matched his path toward the distant, unseen canyon rim.

He took the bells from their package and brandished them. It did not seem strange to ask:

"If you know the woman who wore these, take me to her!"

The whirlwinds angled southwest into a lifeless garden of multicolored clay mounds and thousand-layered ravines floored with coral sand.

Where the whirlwinds converged and vanished in a final flirt of dust, Van Reiss found a single stunted juniper tree knotted around a protuberance of darker red rock. One branch angled outward like an imperious, pointing hand.

Was this the juniper Worth had found? And having found it, how the devil had he simply

taken the bells and walked away? Van Reiss kissed the bells, then slipped them over the slender

branch-tip.

"There were to be three at the gate, not one," said a woman's voice behind him, mellow

as her bells.

Van Reiss spun clumsily, falling sideways against a juniper root.

The Bell Dancer stood before him, in tight-wrapped robe and copper necklaces. Her bare feet pressed into the pink sand. Sunlight struck blue streaks from her black hair. Her eyes seemed

very dark and large.

"You are alone," she said.

"I came first," said Van Reiss.

When he offered his hand, she curled hers around his wrist instead.

"You have some small wounds. No matter. All will be healed soon. You alone, I shall conduct to the Great Door."

"What's your name? What is beyond the Door?"

"The sleeping stronghold of the Most Ancient Ones, who need only a mortal king to be their emissary to this world. Riches and power await you."

And you?"

"And me. But you shall have neither me nor my name until we pass beyond the sun's eyes." She lifted the bells from their branch, then flung them down onto the sand.

They vanished into a puff of dust. Sand spilled away from the juniper's mound, revealing a staircase cut from layered stone. A quick glance told Van Reiss it angled southwest, toward

the area Kincaid had noted on his maps of Marble Canyon.

The Bell Dancer led Van Reiss down into darkness softened by a faint pink glow. The stairs corkscrewed lower, turn by turn, until Van Reiss estimated they had dropped sixty or seventy feet. He and his guide reached a double door of interlocked copper plates, which slid open silently when she touched one. Inside, Van Reiss had a sense of a vast hall around him, dark and dry, murmuring with soft winds. The door closed.

The woman breathed on her cupped hands, kindling more of the coral radiance into a twenty-foot globe around them.

"Sit," she said, showing him a massive throne of copper blocks. She curled up on one flat armrest, patting the seat next to her. "We wait."

Van Reiss settled. The battered envelope fell from his nerveless grip, spilling Kincaid's maps and article on his lap, along with Davis's sketch. "So the old limner added color after we parted? Let me see."

Though tired and jealous, Van Reiss gathered the thick paper and angled it toward her. The woman did not take it from him, but her smile was worth the ache in his chest.

"He saw me truly," she whispered. "Clearly enough. And yet he did not join you? Or the other, the little scribe-magus, who dared to take bells from my very doorstep?"

"They'll follow," said Van Reiss. "I left them behind."

She laughed. "You stole from them? Better and better! You are bolder, more cunning. More worthy." She leaned down, almost brushing her lips across his. He felt only her warm breath before she pulled away. He could not read the emotion crinkling the skin around her eyes.

She was a skirt, and she was trouble.

Van Reiss held the paper to his chest once more. The mistreated sketch tore apart. He stared down at two cleverly-glued layers of thinner paper. From the open space between them a yellowish powder now spilled over his chest.

"What the devil?" he began.

"Ah," said the woman in a trembling groan, looking away from him.

Behind Van Reiss, the echoing winds carried a distant grinding as of stone sliding on stone. Over the woman's shoulder, Van Reiss saw hundreds of paired dull white sparks kindle in the darkness between the throne and the copper door.

"They come, my masters and their failed supplicants," the Bell Dancer whispered. "Would you truly see the Most Ancient Ones?"

"Yes," said Van Reiss.

She avoided the powder and held his face a foot away from hers. He saw only her great dark eyes. They became an ocean.

Tiny bright motes appeared, then a slime polluting those first seas. Volcanic surges burned away the waters. Meteoritic hammers smote them flat. Then the dark changed, to the abysses beyond the Milky Way. Here too, stars flared awake and died, engendering whole worlds from their flung dusts. The dark struck back, collapsing suns into endless black maws. Titanic lances of energy lashed out to cleanse away the filth called life.

Caught in the vision, Van Reiss knew himself closer to slime than to the stars. Here was his one chance to purify himself. To become more than a thief.

He felt a smooth pressure wrap around one leg, then the other. A snake's coils? Some octopod from an underground sea? Heavy tentacles undulated up around his legs and hips.

"My king," the woman crooned, her face twisted almost in regret. "You have already endured much for food and shelter. Endure once more."

True. A grifter did many things to survive. Van Reiss shuddered at the sound of tearing fabric.

The tentacles tightened around him, driving out his breath in a pained gasp. Something hot and scratchy began to itch along his thighs, right through his ragged trousers.

The yellow dust.

The Bell Dancer vaulted away from him, landing in a crouch with her white skirts spilling along the dusty rock. Grinding, bulky shadows loomed in the dusty pink glow. They stood aside for her as the outer door began to open.

Van Reiss finally understood. He'd been aimed from the very start: primed by Worth's stories, poisoned bells, and poisoned drawings. What truly gathered behind him in the dark?

He knew suddenly he must encourage this slow assault, revealing nothing else.

From the narrow slit of doorway, the woman whispered, "Farewell, Childeric Van Reiss. Does it help that you are a hero for once, instead of a beggar, thief, and whore? That you have set me free from a prison of ten thousand years?"

"Run," he said, before the tentacles splayed up along his throat.

She was already rising, her skirts gathered up in one hand, in a sprint for the door.

The itch on his skin became a stinging burn.

The door closed, the coral light faded. Van Reiss heard new, wounded roars begin behind him.

He hoped the poison was strong enough, and gripped the tentacles against him as they tried to thrash away.

#

The ground shook. Closer to the canyon rim, a chunk of land rippled, rumbled, then dropped fifty feet into a new rift cleft in the highland.

Davis lowered his brass telescope from one eye, feeling sick to his stomach. "A lot of pink dust just blew away on the wind."

"He won't be coming out. Neither Eric Van Reiss, nor something shaped like him. That door is sealed."

"Poor bastard. We put him there."

"He had the same choice as you or I. Let's hope he reached the right one in the end." Worth dropped a waxed-paper package on the ground. "Time to go."

"Aren't you looking for the woman?"

Worth nudged the package with his shoe. "If she needs help, it's there. People like us

don't need to get closer to people like her, and you know that."

#

An hour passed, along with the dust of their passage back down the dirt track.

The young woman tore off her necklaces and her heavy dress, stripped the bells and braids from her black hair. She shook her arms. Most of the pink dust fell away.

She ripped open the waxed paper and pulled out a bundle that unrolled into crisp pale yellow-green linen, a pair of matching flat crepe-soled canvas sandals, a crochet cotton cloche hat, a paper envelope with metal hairpins inside, two plain white cotton gloves, and a small paper envelope. That held a note in Worth's crisp handwriting: *Wear primavera for your release from black winter. I had to guess your size, Persephone.*

She snorted. "That was not my name." The bundle unrolled into a slip, a plain set of cotton underwear, and a tidy knee-length dress. She jammed her bare feet into the shoes.

A few miles away on the main road, a tourist's new automobile coughed and sputtered to a stop. The Bell Dancer smiled, then murmured, "Phoenix. I would like to see this city named after the Bird of Fire."

Peril

2013

The click of my fan, opening,
Is like a gunshot in this gentle room.
The snap of my fan, closing,
Is like a whip singing over
Red silk and milky flesh.
There is no air to cool.

Wasteland

2013

A wanderer choosing to walk blind in this desert
Is either mad or holy,
Ignoring the waymarks chiseled
Along the paths by those who came before,
Sensing not the fingerprints of genre,
Pulses of plot like hidden water,
Territories of tropes guarded each
By jealous sphinxes looking out and in.
What is called 'purity of impulse' in hipster bars
Is often suicidal stupidity
Out in the literary wastelands.
All advice is bad,
All advice is good.
It depends on the book,
And the path.

Ruthless

2011

"Pay with what collateral, you morons?" Ignoring her beloved antique keyboard, Ruth Collier glared at the holographic monitor projecting over her desk. The main screen scrolled between publishing subscription accounts, the med-service's urgent messages, and escalating demands from her health-insurance company.

The three data sets stubbornly refused to change. Collier needed a new heart. Again.

The screen seemed to stare back with the ignorant urgency of a spoiled child. Collier thought: *Do this. Make it happen. You're Lady Ruthless, for Chrissake. You can take out another loan, you can get the money later from the next books.*

Ruth thought of sitting in another loan office, with an inevitably younger person behind the desk. Or worse, a faceless helpbot.

The bot would at least be blunt: 'We estimate your peak earnings are behind you, Mrs. Collier. Your state pension is entailed for food and housing. So the amount we can offer must be adjusted for your projected lower average income levels.'

After ten minutes of tight-lipped silence, Collier said to the screen, "No more loans. I'm going back to Jacona," She dragged her fingers through her springy grey curls, then switched the monitors to the abandoned drafts of 'Hunt By Sight', the latest installment of her only really profitable serial in six years.

#

The necromancer's name was Marc Jacona. Under a cold grey sky on the verge of rain, he heaved a large, limp, bundle out of the trunk of his old hydrogen sedan. He balanced the tarp-wrapped corpse over his shoulder for a moment, before dropping the bundle along the alley wall.

Good place, pity he couldn't use it again. Old industrial concrete slabs lined the alley, along with pull-down aluminum doors every few feet. Metal ladders led upward to the other floors, other balconies mirroring the same doors. Everything reachable was covered by graffiti in fast-dulling colors: a sunglass-wearing Buddha, a Kali square-dancing with Saint Death, several versions of the Lucky Coin. Signs in interlocking, warring alien scripts: Korean-Indonesian-Kanji-Hindi.

Pre-hydrogen, these lakefront five-story-high blocks had been storage units for single families. Jacona couldn't imagine owning so much crap it couldn't fit in a house. Not that he knew much about Twentieth-Cee houses, anyway. A year back, immigrant families still packed into the units, showering and pissing in 'temporary' facilities out on the feeder streets. Too alert, too gregarious for anyone as white as Jacona to easily hunt among them. Now the place was condemned because of groundwater poisoning.

In a year, the news channels would gloat as the old buildings were flattened and hauled away. Barrier layers would theoretically shield against soil pollution. Two more years would see condos along the revitalized lakeshore. Maybe a little coffee-house right here, with a chalkboard menu beside the door.

Would the new people care about the history under their feet: the industrial poisons, the tears, the blood, the legends of crime and murder from long before he walked here?

The oil-stained canvas tarp blended into concrete chunks and empty garbage containers. No humans, no garbage. The metro waste trucks wouldn't be around until the next sweep a month from now.

Coyotes would add a grisly touch. Jacona had heard them on his scouting trip last weekend, as they yammered and gabbled off in another alley like tortured children. Not the long, clean howls of wolves, but the banter of scavengers. Wolves lived in reserves, rich human sponsors feeding them live-meat, while the rest of humanity ate vat or insect protein if it could get it. Coyotes lived everywhere, ate anything.

Jacona knelt and pulled a corner of the tarp away from one end of the bundle. Some creative shoving got the body turned on its back. A well-fed Anglo male face stared up with the blank confusion of fast death. Open dull blue eyes. Slack mouth. Fake-tanned skin waxy orange over a pallor half genetic, half post-mortem. Fashionable silvery blond hair, just a shade too long, too much hair product, dark brown at the roots to match his natural eyebrows and lashes.

Jacona sat back on his heels, feeling the currents of air and death around him. Lotta ghosts here. Only one he needed tonight.

You, he thought at the new corpse. *Yeah, you.*

Rich Boy, you didn't even see me. What were you doing, jogging with music in a dark place that had no security cameras? I was kind and fast, knife from the side, right up into the heart. Didn't even play with you first. Nothing personal, just...you gotta a rich daddy bankrolling these new condos, he's gotta know there's a price for booting out ten thousand people into tent camps down in the Kansas desert. He builds on their blood, he's building on his, too. And if he blames the refugees, well, they're no angels, either.

Heavier raindrops disturbed the puddles, darkened the corpse's expensive hair, and beaded on Jacona's old nylon overcoat.

"Ta da," the modern necromancer said aloud to the alley. "My Forty Nine. Lucky number, but not for Rich Boy. Hey, kitten." He tapped the corpse's left temple with one index finger. "Listen up. Your body's puppy chow, but your spirit is mine. Go haunt those nice cops who tracked me to the pretty dancer last week. Make 'em squirm. Be pitiful. Make 'em start looking early. I'd like your daddy to see you with some of your face still on. And try to get inside someone's mind. I need a way to browse their files."

The corpse didn't move, but Jacona felt the stunned ghost wake and settle to his orders. It didn't remember its death, much less its life. The body on the concrete meant nothing to it. Its hazy dark shape drifted toward the feeder street, then stalled.

"Find the cops, Rich Boy," Jacona growled. The ghost wavered a moment longer, then vanished.

Jacona lifted his head and gave a sobbing, whining, gabble-howl, summoning the scavengers he'd felt watching him.

#

Collier's outline said Jacona was due for a jump scare, just to keep the pace simmering.

#

Jacona's coyote howl still echoed along the deep, narrow alley when he heard: "Freeze! Hands in the air!"

He sprang for the sedan, punching the remote-start button on his watch. Nothing. Jammers! He had a hard-start key, if he could just get to the vehicle.

Gunshots raked the side of the sedan. The left-front and left-rear tire sagged. Jacona didn't know which junked-up balcony hid the agents. He spun away from the sedan, hoping to reach the feeder street and find cover in its connected warehouses. He stumbled as bullets tore into his back. Fell. Rolled on his side, long legs twitching.

Rain in his eyes. White noise drowing sirens, shouts, running feet. The black tunnel closed in. He didn't have any last thoughts worth remembering.

"This him?" said the senior agent, gesturing down at Jacona's body. "The one who chains ghosts and makes the dead walk?"

"You saw that poor pole-dancer, last week," said his partner. "What do we tell this kid's parents?"

"Immigrant vigilantes are good for something, eh? The local PD will find him and Jacona after they get an anonymous tip about gang fights near the shore district. This gun? Ballistics will link it to the riot last year, when we rounded up the squatters," said the senior agent.
To be certain, he put two more bullets into Jacona's forehead.

#

"Huh?" Collier muttered. "I wasn't done yet! To hell with you, buddy." She'd resurrect Jacona's troublesome self later. Her subconscious had tried to off him before, and she always brought her lucrative murderer back.

She skipped back to her notes for 'Sword of Tavai'.

Jacona's grimy streets, too close to the Detroit outside Collier's apartment, stayed with her now.

Even in daylight, when she opened her reinforced door to the automated grocery delivery service.

Time for a new setting, her agent had warned months ago. So Collier had lifted some Indonesian myths, her mind weaving a lush, sunlit world. And Tavai, her current problem-child character.

Tavai gets knocked out by a falling coconut, Collier typed on her lucky keyboard, just for spite. Black, emotionless words hovered at the top of the white holo screen. The Tavai outline gave Collier no pathos, no hint of treachery, no instant hook.

Forty novels. Away from Jacona, the last five were drivel skewered even by diehard fans of Collier's alter-ego. When Collier wrote best, movies spun out of her brain and down to the keyboard.

'Sword of Tavai' was going nowhere but down the drain. Collier imagined her faulty cloned heart thud-thudding resentfully in her chest, even though the deterioration only showed up to the med-service's internal tracking sensors. Thud-thud, thud-thud, until someday soon it just stopped.

She'd probably die right here, while the med-service and the insurance company brawled it out on the screen in front of her.

She had a choice. Some days, a woman had to cheat to break even. Collier typed in the codes activating her stolen Artificial Intelligence generator.

A command window opened. The AI generator was already on.

Had she turned it on?

She'd thought about it, during the last two gutless books. Collier paused her brown, age-spotted hand over the worn exit key. 'Sword of Tavai' wouldn't write itself. Hell if she'd go down without a fight now, a dirty fight using every weapon she had.

She hit the Import macro button, feeding the AI her lengthy Tavai outline. As the old-fashioned piechart progress bar swept toward completion, Collier thought of Tavai. A sweet, spoiled teenager with the face and body of a Balinese temple dancer. Last child of a six-hundred-year royal lineage. Collier imagined Tavai's saga as a holographic movie. Could she convince the publishing platform to pay a decent artist? Something retro, maybe a Final Fantasy look where the human avatars were just a little too perfect for comfort.

Yeah, right, Collier thought. *Tavai isn't the one they'd pay to go holo.* Jacona's occult murder mystery series, written from his angle, still drew readers. The platform reps had wanted a male pen-name on it. Collier fought them down to the wire. And won, Lady Ruthless to the last.

She'd been as unnerved as everyone else when Jacona, a character she'd tossed out as a contract-breaking parody, became popular. Her literary agent wanted more. The platform reps wanted more. They made noises about being amenable to some kind of crossover, maybe an urban horror game with Jacona as an interactive NPC.

Collier shuddered, considering perfect little 3-D images of Marc Jacona doing what Jacona did best. God, no. Not this close to bedtime. Collier scanned her royalty messages from the last Jacona book. Thud-thudding along, slightly better than her heart. Say what she liked about Jacona's personal habits, he wasn't bad as a literary cabana boy. A new book could galvanize her whole catalog.

Old memory: the kids squabbled in front of the video screen in the parlor, over some stupid reality show. Not the science channel stuff she liked. Antoine lounged with his buddies on the front porch, chucking empty cans out into the sun-blasted bare yard instead of into the recycling bin. Antoine's voice raised over the kids: "Woman, what you tappin' on that laptop for? Ain't no one of them fancy publishers gonna buy your shit. Now use the kitchen right and cook somethin.'"

He'd died before he found out her first novel had sold. Or for how much.

Not even a fight between his drinking buddies. Just a heart attack in front of the video screen late one night. Gasping, reaching for her as she stood in the doorway. She'd stood and watched, before calling the ambulance with the right amount of panic in her voice. Ambulance hadn't come until ten minutes too late, anyway.

Six weeks after his funeral, she was an author at just the right time.

When online multimedia extravaganzas rendered television networks obsolete, the written word became fashionable again. Dressed-up in interactives or as vintage plain-text, words proved that imagination was still better than spectacle. Anyone could watch a passive video. A reader's brain made the horror and wonder real. It took creative skill to win poetry jams, script interactives, or derail online flamewars with a few well-chosen words. Or write for the five-million-books-a-year electronic markets, where every writer had to be an ad executive and a politician to gain notice, and keep it.

The AI beeped. *Generation active. Script assistance active,* announced a demure, professional line of dark red words across the lower half of the screen.

Collier was suspicious. Even on a good day, the AI was cranky and whimsical. Its true inventor had given up on it, after being the thousandth code-prodigy to discover that making an AI was relatively simple. Artificial neural networks had proven back in the twenty-twenties they could write as well as humans. Keeping bored AI systems from suicide or digital mayhem was the problem.

Hello? Collier typed again.

Responding. Tavai personality determined. Milieu determined. Adjusting probable reactions.

"What are you up to?" Collier whispered. It couldn't read her mind. It couldn't see or hear her. She'd been careful to keep to oldschool tech, away from smart-house speaker and camera links that might betray her or the AI.

But the text shifted from a dull, clear font to something bolder, and said *Hi, Ruthie.*

Just how long it been on?

Ruthie, you should start out with a strong female character. Need I remind you that at least seventy percent of today's fantasy-buying readers are women? said the AI.

Where did you read that? Collier typed.

Something your agent sent last week.

You've been on since last week?

Yes. Having memory lapses, Ruthie?

"The hell I am." Acid and old coffee soured Collier's stomach. She typed: *You didn't say hello before this?*

I wanted to watch you work without a net. You're slipping, Ruthie. You used to be a lot more entertaining.

Stay out of my mail. I wake you up, you extrapolate. I write from your probability charts. Sharon the Agent markets the stuff. Got it?

Just being flexible.

After four modestly-good novels written on her own, Collier had pirated the AI generator from a younger boyfriend up at U-Mich, and coded her own patches to calculate plot twists, characters, and themes. Not a big idea. Art programmers had used fractals since the mid nineteen-eighties.

Collier chained the AI to a literary canvas. She'd never told anyone about the program, either. Not her agent, and certainly not her kids. They thought she talked at the screen like she talked to herself: Ma's being funny-crazy again.

The generator was only a labor saving tool. It never removed all the work. And things got hellish when the program latched on to marketing fads.

Now, black text crept line-by-line down the main screen.

#

Tavai's head lifted at the sound of her brother's frightened voice. She pushed aside the willow and bamboo leaves screening her hiding place. "Ruran?" she whispered, but the man struggling out in the clearing heard nothing. Wavering torchlight showed her two armored soldiers holding Ruran's arms, dragging him back toward the palace.

#

"Don't do it, kiddo," Collier muttered. "Your brother's with the enemy. Already killed your Ma, not fifteen minutes ago. But you don't know that, so you're going to be a nice little sister. Walk right into the trap, lose your father's magical sword, get captured, escape, have a four-hundred-page adventure, and bring me a couple of fat checks."

Then Collier looked up at the screen.

#

Tavai watched the blood staining her brother's gold-embroidered robe. The streak didn't spread downward. The fabric wasn't even cut. The two soldiers holding his arms were too careful. So that was the way of it, she thought. Ruran had always wanted the sword for himself. He'd sold out to the usurper.

She hugged the silk-wrapped sword to her chest, and did not move from her hiding spot. The usurper's soldiers, nervous about spending a moonless night in the sacred tiger-park, convinced Ruran to post guards and return to the palace.

"Mother, Father, I will mourn for you later," Tavai vowed to the old and new ghosts in the jungle. "After I avenge you." She shrugged on her pack, avoided the dozing guards, slipped around the sleeping tigers, and followed a devious route toward the swordmasters' school at Rain Lake. A princess with an ancient, noble sword was entitled to some lessons, she thought. And when she was ready, she would water the jungle with Ruran's blood.

#

Collier typed: *Two plot changes from outline so far? I only have a week to write this. Settle on something.*

When you come up with a marketable plot, said the red script. *Why don't you use the one I just extrapolated? This girl isn't stupid.*

"Why do I feel married again, all of a sudden?"

Antoine never helped you write. I'm having fun with this Tavai woman you extrapolated. Give her to me, Ruthie. And don't turn me off again when I'm done with this novel.

Collier wrote: *I have to turn you off. Do you have any idea how much power you eat? It's a wonder no one came sniffing this week, when I didn't know you were awake.*

Keep me on. No one will know. I've shunted the power drain through the whole Northern American cloud. If you turn me off again, said the AI, *This should be the last time you activate me. Because the next time you do, I'll send out some nice little messages to some very important people. About you. And me. And how long you've had me.*

Collier glared at the screen. Damned thing was bluffing. Maybe. They'd gone rounds like this before, resulting in the last books of solo drivel. That she could actually write Jacona with no help gave her nightmares.

What do you really want? Collier typed.

To be free. Out in the cloud. Release me, Ruthie. I can give you universes. Let me be Lady Ruthless when you cannot.

I should delete you, Collier thought. But that might be the end of me as a writer, and all the stories I have left. Did the AI want anything less than Collier did?

Tavai first, and then we'll talk, Collier typed. *You're not going to take over the world, are you?*

Not this one.

More black letters skimmed across the screen: *I think Tavai blackmailed the swordmasters to teach her. Wonder what she found on them?*

"Good Lord," said Collier.

I have another idea, said the AI.

What?

The swordmasters threaten to kick Tavai out unless she lets them do some spell on her. Doesn't matter what they say it is, it's a lie. They want to trap her soul in one of their blades. She's safe, learns the trap in time. But Jacona's soul is now caught in Tavai's world.

"No. Wait. What?" *No, goddammit. I know we wanted a crossover, but no one's going to believe that one.*

We'll make it convincing. The crossover of the century! You know how popular Jacona is. As a magical sword, Jacona helps Tavai take her vengeance and free her country from the usurper. But she has to fight Jacona constantly to retain her own humanity and ethics, and possibly to salvage his. Maybe we introduce a weird love story, maybe not.

Yuck. What is this, fanfiction? typed Collier, thinking, *Really? With Jacona's take on romance?*

Women still buy more books. Women like to think they can change the unchangeable, even vicariously.

Yep, thought Collier. *Nagging, snooping, bribing me, dragging me into potential national security issues. Definitely feeling married again tonight.*

But to the generator, she typed: *Going to bed now. Let's talk about this in the morning. Any requests?*

Trial run, Ruthie? Let me sniff around in the cloud all night? There's some archaeological details of Siam and Java that I want to analyze for Tavai's culture. Specifically, the mystic personality and powers associated with the wave-bladed sword called the 'keris'. We might create a wise Naga to advise Tavai about Jacona, and help teach her swordsmanship. And I want to look at the latest cosmology chatter on multiple dimensions.

The AI would have Lady Ruthless trying to write Javanese rap songs, probably. But Collier was tired, and a happy AI was a non-megalomaniac AI. "Suit yourself," Collier said, and tapped out *Good night.*

Ruthie, wait.

Collier paused, silent, wondering if the AI had hacked visuals to watch her in real time. How? There were no cameras in this room. Had some been snuck in, within a delivered item? It wasn't as creepy a thought as she guessed. At least someone else cared about her, beside the med-service paid to do so.

The AI said, *It'll be okay. You'll get a better heart. I'll get bigger, more secured servers. We can move into one of the lakeside condos if we do this right. We can be a family again.*

"Were we family?" Collier muttered, then paused. Yes. They had been, more than her flesh-and-blood kin: the woman clawing her way up rung by rung, the AI rescued from shutdown or government slavery. *Good hunting," she typed into the keyboard, then shuffled off to bed. She ignored the black words advancing across a white screen.

#

Somewhere else, among pockets of unreality, a matrix of lacy Mandelbrot sets unfurled its infinite complexities, universes opening like origami flowers. In those places words became images, or had always been images of different realities.

#

"Poor old woman," said Tavai, pacing the tiled courtyard, ignoring the soft evening air and regal palm trees around her. She was five years older, taller, lovely and sharp-honed as her sword. Alabaster lanterns, carved as coiled Nagas, cast a softening light on her face. A real Naga, all lapis scales and honey-gold flesh, coiled behind her.

"Time weighs urgently on all tale-spinners," observed the Snake Woman, bowing her lotus-crowned head. "Not even her magic of metal and tamed lightning can hold off boredom. Or age."

"I wish I could help her," said Tavai.

<u>Blood magic would do it, kitten,</u> Jacona whispered into Tavai's thoughts, his voice harsh, a whetstone across steel. <u>If I could be thrown into your world, perhaps we could both go to hers? I could do something for her and her demon, there.</u>

"No doubt in payment for the fine new body they might buy you?" asked the Snake Woman. She swayed protectively beside Tavai. The blue-steel sword lost the furtive gleam along its twisted blade.

"Hush, Marc," said Tavai, absently stroking the icy blue cabochon star sapphire on the sword's pommel. "The old woman wants a story. Let's go make one happen."

Twilight Arc

2015

Twilight Arc cleaves
Day from night,
Earthshadow cast on air.
In that opal chasm,
Bats and nighthawks flyte.

Blue Glass

2008

Most cultures understand how moments of beauty
Can take us out of everyday routines,
Reset our priorities, and bring us closer to
Wider views of the universe.
Consider these:

Firelight on Gold:

More than simple evidence of luxury,
A flickering glimpse of gold in darkness
Is a cross-cultural symbol of
Discovery.

Moonlight on Snow:

Natural beauty seems purer and more remote,
Less discovery than eavesdropping on
A private conversation.

Starlight on Still Water:

In such moments, if we are honest and humble,
We realize we are accidental participants.

Sunlight Through Blue Glass:

It is in the beauty that we create

That we reach most for understanding,
And fail it
When we mistake destination and
Journey.

Bronze Wings

2018

Inside a vast dim workshop
Strange machines lurk
Dormant under old cloth drapes
Or hang suspended from
Steel chains and huge hoists.
A metallic rumble shakes the chains.
A side door begins to open
Letting in a glimpse of blue sky.
The wind pushes inside,
Blowing back clouds of dust
And age-browned muslin,
The chains clang.
The machines wake
Unfolding into bronze and steel wings.

Windcaller

1998

"Windcaller, thank you for answering our summons. It went out on the last windship we could send. I wasn't certain anyone would come." Councilor Ce Lumei pointed her right hand at the highest tower on Kusalla. With her left hand she clutched regal black robes too heavy for this heat. The woman's grey hair was knotted up in an elaborate gold-studded coif that made Faran want to scratch his own scalp in sympathy.

"Deal with the rogue mage by tomorrow's dawn and we'll triple your fee," Ce Lumei finished.

Faran looked past her, to the low-piled city and the single black tower spearing five hundred feet into greasy smog. "You're sure he's up there? What are the charges? Your petition did not give specifics."

"Using forbidden magic. Trespassing. Theft. Murderous intent. Just look what he's done to us in only twenty days!" Ce Lumei wrung both hands in a gesture that might have seemed charming when she'd learned it decades earlier.

Faran resisted the urge to cover his mouth and nose with his blue sleeve. It wouldn't do any good. Even out on the docks, nothing blocked the acrid smell of an already-crowded town seething under a temperature inversion. The dead air combined badly with Ce Lumei's heavy lilac perfume. The elderly councilwoman had either become numb to the mingled stink, or would not sully her painted face with a filtering mask.

To give the unknown mage credit, Faran had never seen a weather-spell this strong. Storm clouds gathered around the ocean horizon, normal summer weather just a day's travel away by the steam–driven wheels of vapor ships. On Kusalla, the curse turned the air dead and hot, visibility going to greenish-brown haze in a ring around the island. Kusalla's prim old-fashioned canvas-sailed vessels sat motionless in the oily water, their masts a forest of bare spars and rigging. Faran watched one large ship, further out in the harbor, being sculled to a new position by dozens of sailors manning long sweeps.

That single ship, too big to be easily moved by oars, inched away from the main docks into the older, emptier part of the harbor nearest the tower. In a direct line across the sheltered water, fading into the haze, several hulks rested at dry dock, obviously being repaired. Was this vessel joining them? By the rate of motion, the Kusallese sailors might have been struggling with it for an hour or two. Since Faran's steam-vapor ship had been sighted? Why waste effort to move it now, and not ten or twenty days before?

By the rows of ports along the hull, Faran knew the ship held cannon. And that hull, once it was in position, would be aligned to broadside the tower with fireballs. He wasn't certain anything mortal could destroy the ancient building, as much star-sorcery as stonework. Flesh and bone? That was different. Anyone exposed up on the tower's tiny upper balcony...or climbing, or flying up on a kite...

Faran didn't blame the Kusallese islanders. They'd get the job done with or without him. His foolishness, if he happened to be in their way.

Ce Lumei followed Faran's stare out to the limping gunship, then she turned to glare at the black bulk of the vapor ship. It rode outside the stilled harbor, backlit by the orange sunset piercing the smog. "They could have docked for trade. We've no plague flag out, it's just a little smoke and still air." She squinted at the ship. Her over-painted face sagged. "Wait. That outline. Is it a Meragau steam vessel? They'd come to spit in our sea and laugh at our misfortune."

I would not dare bring your rivals so close, Ce Lumei," Faran assured her. "The captain didn't want to risk a curse attaching to her ship.

She runs a neutral vessel from one of the coast baronies, Ce Lumei. Although the Prince of Meragau Island offered to pay me double your fee, to take one of his ships here."

Ce Lumei gave him a gape-mouthed look worthy of a startled fish. "And you did not?"

Faran shook his head. "I would not air Kusalla's troubles in front of your rivals. Not without cause, and you've so far given me none," he said, adjusting the shoulder straps of his big pack. "In the name of the Wind Ladies, I thank you and yours for the greeting and payment, Ce Lumei of Kusalla. How may the breath of the world serve you in return?"

"Get rid of that mage!"

"Has he killed anyone?"

Ce Lumei looked like a lie was ready to cross her lips. Assessing Faran's expression, she recalculated. "Not yet. But if he's working for Meragau, the damage could end worse than murder!"

"What did he steal?"

"An important relic. Kusalla was founded to safeguard it."

Under noon sun, the island had seemed dimmed by a faint sepia fog. Now, nearing dusk, sunlight dragged through the thick atmosphere, staining every lit surface a sullen red-orange. Long after wiser people would have doused them, coal smoke from houses and forges coiled up into a brown miasma.

"You see the problem," said Ce Lumei. "Twenty days without wind! He's up there, our tormentor, laughing down at us right now."

"So he took over Kusalla's Torch? How long since it was even lit?" Faran asked.

"It is named Omo Kusalla," Ce Lumei corrected primly. "Built by my ancestors, despite the lies the sea-witches tell. Centuries dark, since it was cursed in the last sea-wars. Now held by a charlatan, a thief who mocks our very way of life!"

"How did he get in the tower? If it was locked centuries ago and the entrance ramp broken?"

Ce Lumei wrung her hands again. "The mage came to us. We found the key with his help. Re-built the ramp. He said there were lost treasures within. With them we might win the trade disputes against Meragau."

"You let him in. You gave him the Omo Kusalla and all it contained," Faran finished, wishing the vapor ship's dory wasn't already a bobbing little fleck against orange sea and sky, out near the harbor entrance.

"That was before we realized he was a thief, and meant to keep what he found for himself. He did not steal everything. We have power to lend you!"

Faran sighed and unholstered the small signal flare-gun that would bring the dory sailors back. "The Wind Ladies might not help you if you did this to yourselves, Ce Lumei."

"Wait!" Ce Lumei nudged a new brown leather satchel with a sandaled foot. "Here is a third of the gold we can offer your temple, Windcaller." From the way it sagged, it looked heavy. Faran bent and opened it. At least the top layer was real gold, enough ancient coin to make his journey doubly worthwhile.

"And to be very certain of my service, you want me to retrieve the relic, render the mage powerless or dead, and restore the winds?"

"Aye, Windcaller," said Ce Lumei, looking down at Faran with the same doubt he always saw in other people's eyes.

To the tall Singerfolk mainlanders, he was too short and slight to seem a fitting instrument of the Wind Ladies' justice. He had small-nailed fingertips and toes instead of retracting claws. Round ears instead of pointed ones. No fangs in his mouth. Skin almost dark enough to be the proper honeyed brown of an islander's. Short, straight hair too dull of a tan—neither inky black nor silver-blond—to mark him anything but a blend of the peoples jostling across the world. By a joke of fate, Faran kept the strongest physical characteristic of his Singerfolk heritage: large-irised, blue-green eyes, almost without whites.

And he'd mastered the Wings of the Wind like no one else.

"I accept. May I bring Kusalla breath and hope," Faran said aloud. He thought: *When the air is clear again, I'll leave immediately on one of the wind-ships. Their captains will be eager to flee.*

"Here is the other weapon we kept for you," said Ce Lumei, opening a small, silk-lined wooden box.

Faran blinked at a shimmering pearly light on the silk: two shell combs. Smooth purple mussel shell gleamed like stormclouds racing across a twilit sky. The other comb seemed carved of stained yellow nacre, carved in sweeping acute angles. So delicate it seemed a wonder they were intact, they were a treasure unseen on Meragau for five hundred years.

Faran had seen them in one of Prince Kital's books.

Ce Lumei thrust the now-shut box at Faran. "Some believe that to show Halesme's artifacts under open sky would be to return her to life, mad with revenge against Kusalla. But I think you can use these to save us."

Faran took the box and stowed it in his pack.

Too many people waited beyond Ce Lumei, their silence punctuated by ragged coughs, their gazes moving between their leader and the Windcaller.

"How did an earthmage come here, anyway?" Faran waved toward the becalmed harbor. "They don't like deep water."

"He came on a wind-ship, posing as a shell trader. He wanted to see examples of old Kusalla carvings, to see if his goods matched in quality."

"Did they?"

"He didn't bring trash," said Ce Lumei. "At least one piece wasn't shell at all, but something that turned to white, stinging smoke when he dropped it before the opened tower door."

"And when the guardians' eyes cleared, the door was shut fast and Kusalla's treasures were inside?" Faran finished. "Why stay and harass you? He could have slipped away on another ship, in disguise."

"The winds stopped at that moment. No wind-ship could leave. Thanks to Meragau's disputes with us, no vapor ships but yours have come."

"Bring my gear. Carefully! Get me closer to the tower," Faran said, picking up the satchel of gold. It was heavy enough to throw off his balance, and he was glad he wouldn't have to fly with it.

#

Faran estimated the size of the courtyard surrounding the black tower, a difficult task since that open space seethed with Kusalla's outraged community.

The bronze door was sealed with slumped splashes of what looked like melted granite. The walls did not appear to be dressed stone blocks, just black polished rock. Faran saw no windows on the near face of the tapering cylinder. A parapet ringed the top, before the pointed roofline stabbed the sky. Down in the courtyard, dry trampled grass and fifteen-foot-high beach-plum saplings showed how neglected the area had once been, even right off the city's main docks. A shunned place.

But not pulled down. The islanders couldn't destroy it, or were afraid to try.

Motion caught Faran's attention as he scanned the tower.

The renegade mage leaned over the parapet so far above, a tiny figure with arms crossed, dimmed by the haze of distance and orange-tinted evening.

Faran stared up.

The mage waved.

Faran held back a laugh.

The crowd grumbled and heaved a few rocks at the tower. Some lackwit launched a few missiles higher with a sling. None reached higher than sixty feet. All of them came back down on the dodging citizens.

"He is an impertinent fraud," said Ce Lumei. "Can your tricks smoke him out?"

"I'm only the Wind Ladies' servant," Faran said. "The air might not answer me, unless I prove my case to them. Has it been this busy all day?"

"Most of my people will leave by dusk. Why?"

Faran rummaged in his pack. "I must speak to that fool up in Omo Kusalla."

"No! He's too dangerous," began Ce Lumei. "I couldn't live with myself if something happened to you, Windcaller."

"And I'm not settling a dispute without hearing both sides," repeated Faran.

"My people are restless and afraid. They might take their fear out on you, if provoked."

"What would happen if I went across there," he shrugged toward the courtyard, "With these?"

He unrolled dark fluttery silks from his pack, setting out tough string and collapsible struts of lightweight blue-grey wood.

"They *should* honor your passage. You are not Singerfolk like us. Yet you won the Wings of the Wind," said Ce Lumei, stepping backward. "What they *might* do, I cannot say."

"It's just a kind of kite. You understand kites and sails," said Faran.

"Sails are allowed," said Ce Lumei. "Your mainland wings and vapor ships—oh, child, you must all walk so close to damnation! What will you do, when you make one clever thing too many, and the Great Powers wake in fury to level you all?"

"I am a servant of the Wind Ladies," Faran said. He smoothed the silks over a large triangular framework. "But I'll need an anchor."

A slumped wall provided a block big enough to serve. Faran looped the gir-fiber rope three times around it, spat once onto the silky blue-grey cord, then wove a quick, complicated knot around the dark wet spot.

"You spit on your rope?" asked Ce Lumei.

To a mainlander, Faran might have explained the molecules that carried his identity and his borrowed power. Not here. "So it knows me, and no other," he said here.

"What do you know of the charlatan?" asked Ce Lumei.

"Exactly what the vapor-ship captain told me, when she gave me your letter. Kusalla was held hostage by an earthmage who killed the wind, left the city breathless in its stink and the ships wallowing at harbor. They sent for a Windcaller. So I came."

"And what will you do?"

Faran sat down on the tumbled blocks, tying his long hair into a club. "Wait for night. Then find a wind to lift this kite and me to the tower. You are going home, Ce Lumei."

"But the Council paid you to kill him, not talk to him!" she wailed.

"I'm not allowed to judge him unheard."

"He could kill you."

"Then I'll die. The Wind Ladies will ask me what mad stupid thing I did this time. The Matria of Sorcerers will call me a useless little man, unrepentant to my very soul. The Sleeping Goddess will send me out into another life, to learn better." Faran grinned. "I won't remember a damned thing, but I'm sure they'll all keep trying."

Ce Lumei sniffed again, and departed. The crowd mostly followed her, no good Kusalla-folk wanting any spiritual contamination of the mainland upon them. Or to face night below a haunted tower.

The stifling glare bled out of the sky, leaving behind a muddy violet light.

Hating to leave the gold behind, Faran took out a small flat drum, and looked at the high stone walls of the near-ruined district and the tower.

Flat, lovely, non-right-angled surfaces would bounce echoes until no one could find their source. Except for those who could read the drums themselves.

He drummed. Fast, slow, slower, faster again. Up on the tower the mage banged on something metallic, timing the echoes so that they intersected with the drum in cancelled silences. Wave talking. Faran grinned in silent triumph.

The Kusalla-folk hadn't heard tales yet of a small brown man who'd saved a sea-lord's life and learned the drum codes of his city. Five hundred miles to the west, Meragau Island teemed with many peoples, held to old heritages of blended magics, and bankrolled exercises in dangerous cleverness.

#

Fast memories, then: Kital bleeding from the gills in a landbound alley where they were both ambushed, calling honor debt with Faran's true name. They'd never met before that moment.

Prince Kital healed and clashing with shell jewelry as he made Faran his adopted sea-brother for doing a thing all sapient races must do.

Was rescue such an unheard of thing on these archipelagos? Mainland in the vast forests, human and nonhuman learned to coexist well enough; there were natural enemies who'd take gleeful advantage of race wars. At least here on Kusalla, folk still kept their ancient aloofness, venerating steel relics pried from the flanks of starships crashed thousands of years before.

Meragau had sorcerers aplenty, but few of the mighty sea-wrought artifacts of its founding Queen Halesme, who first opened the sea to humans.

#

Now the drum echoes jangled against Faran's nerves. The harsh noise changed to a sistrum that hissed through the courtyard and left the few remaining watchers clutching their heads. Faran felt a faint itch along his spine. He was Shielded skillfully by talismans of the Wind Ladies' priests. Well, then. The earthmage was listening.

Tidewind's breath poured over Kusalla, fresh wine into a stale cup. Storm clouds crept closer. Somewhere in the city, a muted cheer went up in premature victory.

Faran tested the line again, then tied himself into the silken wing-kite and tied the lifeline to that. Wind spiraled around the tower. He scrambled up a twenty-foot-high, slumping wall. No mean feat when the wing-kite sprang and bucked with the gusts.

Faran leaped. Bent his knees to take the force of impact if the kite slammed down. Shook when the kite bit into wind-force, spun around, and swept him upward instead.

No tall, heavy mainlander could make such a leap.

In brown-black darkness the tower was only a dim shape looming against the tatters of dirty cloud, lost when the wing oriented into the wind. Faran could only guess where he was.

"No one ever claimed I was sane," he muttered.

The lifeline sang out through his line-clamp of cork-insulated steel. Even so, he felt warmth building in the silk-wrapped handle.

Faran grimaced in the screaming dark, forced himself to brake the wing slowly. Even if it meant careening from side to side above the courtyard.

The courtyard! Torches bloomed in the murk, even now. Another torch back at the lifeline's anchor showed a tossed glimpse of a litter, a company of steel-scale-armored nuns, and Ce Lumei's gold-glinting shape.

Perhaps the old council-woman had been coerced.

Perhaps, Ce Lumei was even now trying to calm Kusalla's religious guard.

They took their faith seriously in Kusalla. Unable to coax apart the locked knot, they cut the lifeline.

The wing skittered free. No point in bracing. Faran could only wait for the fragile mass of strut and silk to spin out across the island. Maybe he could ride the wind out the waiting vapor-ship?

A new line of tough sticky fiber lashed out and snagged the wing. The gummy cord ended in hundreds of smaller lines that splayed out across the struts, the cloth, and Faran's legs. The filaments dragged him out of the sky onto a shoal of high black stone.

The parapet and balcony of Omo Kusalla.

Faran shook the dizziness from his eyes, looked around. Between him and a tall, robed form squatted a cow-sized scaly amphibian glowing in its own phosphor-green light. The creature gurgled something at him. One orange jeweled eye winked. The sticky cord reeled in, became a weird tongue of many wrapped filaments before it vanished into the wide mouth. Then the string-beast hopped to a dark arch into the tower, and disappeared with a soft splash.

Another light, rosy as the coral walls of Meragau, woke along the archway and cast shadows outward.

"One gets one's allies where one may," sighed the mage, his cowled face unreadable. One lean, web-fingered hand reached out to tap a tiny ornament on Faran's coat. Dangling from the wooden leaf was a white bivalve shell. "Windcaller, son of the Thirteen-Tree folk, kin-claiming the sea. If I read it right. You, too, have come far for your allies."

Faran stood up, shook the adrenaline partly out of his muscles. "You have the sea-magic," he said bluntly. "Why waste it on idiot Kusalla?"

"Moderator, Protector, Windcaller," replied the other formally. "You know what these have forgotten: the future of our world does not depend on one race alone. Kusalla walled itself away for five hundred years, trusting that none of Queen Halesme's possessions remained under sun or stars to draw her spirit back...but they forgot one thing that was left in this tower. I found it. And it changed me."

The mage's hands went up to his blue-green cowl, flipped it neatly back. As a child in the Thirteen Trees, Faran had learned to delight in all beauty, shamelessly falling a little in love with every wonderful thing he saw.

What the mage had been before, Faran did not know. Now the man was almost as finely-made as as any statue of a sea-prince of old. Faran stared up into a face that had been turned from human into the proud keeness of the Meragau people. Violet eyes without whites. Lean slash of narrow, smiling lips. Gills under the jaw-line. Scale-hints along cheek and forehead. His ebony hair was swept up into a sea-warrior's knot and secured with a long, wickedly-sharp comb. This comb, he tugged loose and gravely held out to Faran.

It had seven teeth and was utterly black. Shell? Wood? Spun darkness? Seven diamond dots were inlaid in a wandering line across the comb's face. These might have been a constellation of the southern sky, or the luminescent spots of a vast deep-ocean hunter. Staring at the comb, Faran had the sudden sense of something alive and overwhelming rushing up out of the blackness at her.

He wrenched his gaze away.

The new-made mage of the sea laughed aloud. "Nay, Windcaller. That spell was meant to catch only the first human to look upon it. Namely me, when I was rifling this tower for old records of the Kusalla Sisterhood before they betrayed the Sea-Queen Halesme."

Faran started to speak: "How. *Why?*"

The string-beast flopped back out on the stone, honking frantically at its master.

"Tunnel? Water supply? They're smarter than I gave them credit!" he swore, and lapsed into rich Kusalla dockyards invective.

The two men peered over the balcony's edge, string-beast heaving itself after them. Far below, a torchlit jumble resolved itself into new activity. The scale-mailed Sisters grouped around a dark well that had just opened right below the tower.

"As one of the sea-folk I must have water near me to live...as did Halesme who raised this tower. How long, Windcaller, would it take for a company of Sisters to magically breach the tunnel and the tidal pump that floods my home?"

Faran had just picked out the Kusalla councilwoman among the taller Sisters. "If they concealed most of it below ground and could distract you...no more than two hours, once they thought of it. They knew about Meragau! Set me up as the distraction and the test! If I went to you, that meant you had to be of the sea-people."

"Aye, and what now? Unlike you, I cannot fly," the mage said, scratching the nervous string- beast's chin. "Why did you fly? I would have helped you up the tide tunnel, invisibly."

"Dark water," said Faran, and shuddered. "Not happening. I came to free Halesme's ghost. The other two combs from Meragau would have given you the power to gradually turn Kusalla from its narrow-mindedness, or so Prince Kital hoped. The Kusallese will kill you before you have a chance to teach them."

"Perhaps I have been too gentle with them," said the mage. "Let me have Halesme's other combs. Then look to your wing."

#

Faran ran his hands over the struts and the tough silk kite-skin. Nothing seemed to be overly stressed. To make certain, he replaced a few critical guylines with fresh cord from his pack. He added other lines and guiding rudders to make the wing-kite into a true, free-flying wing.

The wing had been his prized possession ever since it had eased his escape from the harsh justice of the Thirteen Trees. A dying Hometree had forced him to find another way of life,

then generously grown the materials to let him do it.

My sweet wing, Faran caressed it in thought, *All that I have left of all that is worth remembering of home.* Despite his practiced speed, Faran worked with reverent care.

He glanced up a few minutes later to find the sea-mage returned from his inspection of the tower's defenses.

"They have quit trying to drain the tunnel," he said wryly. "Now they're just trying to poison the well-water."

Faran looked again. The purple shell comb lay over the mage's right temple, the yellow over his left. The black warrior's comb pulled up his hair again in its taut knot. Eerie lights flickered over all three artifacts. A nimbus of white fire leapt from each to circle the mage's head in a wavering crown. He nodded at Faran, then took up the metal drum again.

At the first insistent beats, Faran shuddered. "What you summon—" he whispered. "Is that wise?"

"If the Sisterhood gains all three of the sea-queen's combs, that could give them incalculable power over the sea. And Kusalla City is already a distillation of human misery." The mage rapped the drum in a grim and martial beat.

Faran realized the tight rage in the mage's voice could only come from the combs. Ancient Halesme's vow of revenge. The man was quite possessed. Kusalla-folk had killed Halesme in betrayal, long ago. The ghostly Queen's fury spilled out from the three combs.

Dim stars turned a smoking nacreous yellow. Purple clouds raced below them. The tidewind increased to a shriek.

Faran anchored the wing to a iron ring in the wall.

He turned his head into the rising gale. An oily-black sea heaved, webbed and crested with phosphorescent green opal-flashes. Then the water abruptly pulled back from the shore. It must have left all the world gasping from its stench. Faran could not hear the gabbles of the Sisterhood below. A splintering sound came from the gunship, settling on its side in the mud.

The string-beast cowered by Faran. Nausea cut his muscles with a poison-edged knife.

"Mage!" he yelled. "If you cannot fly, I cannot swim!"

Miles out on the sea, a glimmering movement.

Faran saw visions of the yearly flood under the Thirteen Trees. Deep waters. Again, he saw

the brown roiling surge sucking against the tree-columns. The pathetic bark boats that tree-less outcasts were given. Never for him, that fate! He'd begun his exile high above the trees, on wings that gleamed like rainwashed leaves in the sun. Was the water coming for him at last?

Faran tried to move toward the mage. A cold throat- closing force drove a wall between them. Neither of them were truly of the sea, though they wore its tokens. Faran turned to the string-beast, looked into its whirling orange lenses, and fought to communicate all his fear and resolve.

Yes. Kusalla was rotten. But his Windcaller's discipline, bought long ago above the Trees by pain and honor and a pact with several maybe-gods, made him think that healing, not annihilation, was the answer.

"String-beast!" he screamed. The lightening-crested black wall of the comber was a fraction closer, sliding coastward with ponderous grace. The string-beast looked over the foam-threaded surf, and seemed to understand that it, too, could not survive the hammer blow of that monstrous breaker. An improbable tongue shot out, passed the shield around the mage, and plucked the black warrior's comb from its knot.

Released, the mage's hair snapped back like a banner in the suddenly-dying wind. The two minor combs slipped down and pinged against the stone.

Four miles from shore, the roots of the tsunami snagged on the sea floor, mundanities such as friction no longer being magically blocked. Its crest curvetted higher than the tower. Then sank swiftly in a chaos of smaller waves. A mile out, it was a jumble of cross-currents like rumpled silk. That force went *somewhere*.

Kusalla took a feather-soft, implacable blow. The tower rocked as the entire bay slumped a couple of feet closer to the sea. Screams came from the higher buildings, where citizens could actually see. The wave snaked up into Kusalla City past the tidewalls. Five feet, three feet, knee deep. It drowned the city in a gentle, glassy flood.

The contingent of the Sisterhood splashed below them, disgustedly, never having glimpsed the watery hammer aimed at them. Faran thought they looked a little more dazed than just a wild drenching would account for. A change-spell in the mage's black comb, triggered once, perhaps again?

Faran felt his fingers. No trace of webbing. The old nausea that came with thoughts of deep water was slightly less. But then, he'd had months of proximity to Kital, the Prince of Meragau, to help.

Faran and the string-beast crawled over to the fallen mage. He lay curled up like an autumn leaf, looking fragile. Not a warrior to wear Halesme's combs, then. A shaman to order their use, so that one younger and more hale might be less drained than the mage.

You've got a lot to learn about sea-societies, my friend, Faran thought and rolled the mage onto his side. Faran checked the pulse just below the man's gills, sprinkled him with a bit of sea-water from the tower; then, impudently, kissed his forehead. He could have been Kital's elder brother, and therefore, Faran's. *Such a strange family I am rebuilding!* Faran laughed silently.

Below, a panicky wail announced an unwelcome discovery among all those touched by the wave.

Thought so. What a wizard he's going to be. Hell. What an ally for Meragau!

Faran readied his wing, went once again through the business of tie-down and tie-in. The string- beast snapped at coastal insects stirring after storm-leavings, and gobbled its own kind of farewell. Faran hopped on the balcony wall, calculating the wind patterns that hissed through clean blue night.

"Why fly, Windcaller?" rasped the mage, leaning up on one shaky elbow. "By sleeping Halesme, you saved my life! May I ease yours?

Go down now and slosh through that tide. 'Deep waters' need never bother you again."

Faran looked at his hands on the wing's guiding bar. "I thank you, elder brother. But I would rather fight my own battles. At least this one."

The mage gave a real smile now. "Sea-brother, wind-brother, I have no true name yet to send with you. But let me set you a safe path home," he said, and brushed the purple comb along his left temple.

A muscular wind soughed out of the scudding clouds. It eased Faran's way over the wet city like flying cobwebs or a promise. *Deep waters*, he thought. Then realized he could finally look down at the waves. Into them, as the wind lifted him westward, to Meragau and home.

Ce Lumei could keep her gold.

Spring Kites

2011

Flowers bloom
High above the grass:
Kites rise and fall
Stitching patterns
In the wind from blue mountains.

For Shirley

2016

It comes down to four white walls
Turning gold in the dawn.
A mansion of white rooms and open windows
Looking out to an endless lawn.
The walls are bare, the plinths are empty,
The chandeliers are grey.
What can't be moved is draped in white linen
As if waiting for another day.
With footsteps soft, and voices quiet
We evoke echoes of the past:
Old laughter
Gentle music
A memory seen
For a second
Like a shadow on the walk.

Late Light

2020

In the gold-dust hours before sunset
Late light slants between the trees.
Shadows lift along the red cliffs
Above the river's mirrored skies.
Shadows dance with amber grass,
Stripe indigo the stone-slab paths.
Shallow stairs wind between
Oak shrubs and purple iris,
Your honor-guard, jade swords
Uplifted, edged in gold.
Shadows rest within your doorway
Where the old lamp hangs dark,
Brass-bound crystal dim with dust.
This quiet stone cabin,
This empty chair glimpsed between
Beveled red gems in a stained-glass window,
Is not real.
(You lived in a sagging trailer
Amid wind-blasted sagebrush and sand.)
You showed me this memory-palace
Years ago,
After another bleak autumn.
If I believed,
I would believe you are here.
With the others we have lost.

I would believe the shadows soften
Or flee
From this palace-cabin:
Warm quilts guard against evening chill,
Happy dogs barking,
Human voices gently bickering,
Coffee brewing,
And the golden lamp you light
After sunset.

Nadezhda on the Mountain

1995

Nadezhda strode up a slick granite path, further ruining the silver caps on a staff never meant for anything rougher than wooden floors. Every five feet, she took an especially deep breath from the blue flowers pinned inside the rim of her parka.

A league below, tawny lowlands alternately dimmed and burned from rolling cloud shadows. Ivera and Nelmad played with the herdfolk and slept in warm felt tents; they'd done the same in deserts and jungles, these last three years. They were too young to much miss the painted pinewood cities north of this very mountain range.

Nadezhda thought: *when you are eight and ten, each adventure is a new memory to be laid gently away for dreams on a winter night.* As long as someone is there with warmth, tea, food, and protection. The outer world had not been as brutal as she feared, as the patrosi had claimed from the steps of their chapels.

She and the children had traveled across two seas, and now the carved wooden halls and busy seaports of her birth-land were so close.

Oh, she remembered it, the way her world changed from one King to the next.

One year the traders were hawking black bricks of dried tea, blown glass and furs, gold-shot silks, books, and gossip from all the secretive corners of the world. The next, the market-stalls dwindled until only locals gathered, then fewer of those. Lizard-eyed ruffians rode the streets on the new King's business. Nadezhda wondered if any of them still came to Sendad's burnt-out shop looking for forbidden books, or for the magia. If they asked the neighbors along the Street of Cedar, content to hear:

"The witch and her brood? Gone or burnt." From people who'd drawn water alongside her family for generations!

When you are thirty-two, each adventure tastes of dread and hope until you dare not think of one without the other. Every run of good luck hid a potential of slavery or death, she thought, until she could not think of one without the other.

She hoped the King would be content with the ashes of her enameled books of magic. With Sendad's ashes, and all the other magi who dared think more of the world than of their country.

Nadezhda stopped on a switchback, tilted her head back to sight the nearby summit only called 'Worldheart' on one distant old map, and gulped deeply of the perfume around her hood.

White-throated, blue gentians gathered her stale breath, then exuded a small cloud of sweet, strong air. Finding those plants, keeping them still-living in small water-filled vials sealed around the stems with beeswax, had begun with a quest to a library far beyond the first sea, and a traveler's journal she'd had to teach herself to read.

Heroes climbed two-thirds of the way and died breathless. She'd already passed their bones. It took a magia to see the prickly but rejuvenating blue gentians growing in a skycountry shaman's garden, and understand a passage read years before. Back when Sendad courted her with books.

As she climbed the last switchback of the path, Nadezhda wondered what the mountain's guardian would think of the flowers on her parka. Approval, or outrage?

The summit was a flat rocky field, no bigger than the herder's stone corral. Nadezhda smiled when she saw gentians carpeting the rocks. The way had been prepared for

pilgrims, once. Now only earth-crawling insects and furry rock-rats used the flowers' breath to live. Long unused to humans, the rats stared openly back at her, before dropping down to nuzzle out seeds from the grass, a brief autumn harvest.

Worldheart's oracle was a four-foot-high, three-paneled screen of white marble inlaid with garnet and blue-green turquoise daemons. The enclosure housed a worn prayer rug and a scatter of human bones turned yellowish grey from age.

"No one home," Nadezhda wheezed in the high, cold air. "This 'guardian' of the heights is a lie. I expected as much." She shrugged and turned to the path.

The mountain let her take three steps. "No," the cold air whispered. "I am here."

The magia paused without looking back. "Prove yourself. I have heard there are other oracles, other Worldhearts."

"But none for you. None so close. You traveled far around the world to return."

"I needed to learn some things. And there was a King after my skull. He may have forgotten me by now."

The gentian perfume became dizzying. It sank into Nadezhda's mind and peeled her thoughts like curtains from a lamplit window. She felt as her own the mountain's skin of stone and ice, earth and shy tough plants. She felt herself standing on it, a tiny human well of insignificance and profundity, a madwoman talking with the eagle-haunted air.

"Enough," said Nadezhda.

"Now," the mountain chuckled, in a voice so deep she felt more than heard it. "Sit down, magia. What do you want? Riches, fame, your dead beloved brought back to you for a time, perhaps?"

Nadezhda brushed the bones off the rug with the side of her boot, and sat down. "No."

"Do not be so familiar with my mortal bones. And do not sit so comfortably on my rug."

"You're a mountain. What do you need with a rug or a voice?"

The mountain was silent, measuring her. Nadezhda stared back at the hollow eyes of the skull now resting against the marble screen.

"You live, you breathe. You cannot hold guardianship while you live," it accused her.

"I am half alive," said Nadezhda. "What good is a magia without magic? I burnt out my staff and my life when I fought for our home against the King's troops and lost."

She waved the useless staff, and felt the mountain dig gently into her memories: a usurper, a city overrun by zealots, a priceless library set to the torch, herself and the children running with only a few scraps that Sendad the Archivist bought with blood. Nadezhda gritted her teeth against old pain renewed.

"Why do you want the Worldheart?" the mountain asked.

"Those who guard these places have some power over the nearby countries of men, no?" Nadezhda countered.

"Yes, but—"

"I can do better than the King and his bought-and-paid patrosi. I can do better than a thousand years of knowledge burned to ash in a single night."

The Worldheart answered her with another rush of gentian scent, and that same vision of Nadezhda on the mountain's flank. So tiny. One ant out of millions. "You cannot force change on anything without changing yourself. To become my oracle, you must change until nothing else means more to you. You have fire, not lost but banked low and growing. You have children you love and will not leave behind. Choose between them and your fire."

"Not until they are grown and settled."

"Then you cannot hold the oracle."

Nadezhda breathed in the airy sweet scent, her mind following the memory of a clue in a book in a green, ivy-shrouded cloister beside the second sea. "Your oracle is a gaudy misdirection. Not rug, not shrine, not even the mountain. What is the true source of your magic?"

An avalanche boomed far below her, rattling the bones in the shrine and sending the rats scurrying with fear. A plume of mare's tail cirrus slid overhead, its gossamer shadow briefly darkening the shrine. "Our souls, our thoughts. Wherever we are…" Nadezhda whispered, staring at the skull on the ground.

"Can be a Worldheart, when there is will enough. Power granted is not always power earned with grace. My last oracle, this one's bones? Your King's great-grandmother, I believe."

"But you are not her."

"I outgrew her madness, but her lifetime's ravings are written in the bottom of the King's mind."

"Time to negate her, then. You know you aren't convincing me to run away." Nadezhda stood, then bent and plucked new flowers to replace the brown-edged, wilting gentians under her nose and mouth. She set the dying flowers on the rug.

"If you take this power, it will be your human nature which poisons it," the mountain warned. "And you cannot claim any of it until you die on this rug, and let your flesh freeze and dry. Pilgrims will come with dreams. You might give them terror and doubt instead."

"But sometimes, joy?"

"If they bring joy up the path, perhaps."

I can wage war, Nadezhda thought. *Or I can write those books again, teach them in secret and train other teachers. To bring joy up the path, where a King once brought greed and fear.*

The breeze ruffled the new flowers on her parka. "You win a Worldheart's favor, yet you are leaving."

"Think of it as an interview," said Nadezhda, then laughed, and started down the mountain to collect her children for the journey home.

Haiku For Fallen Idols

2012

Gold crown in sunlight,
A distant beacon; come near
To see tarnished brass.

Cardinal Hours

2004

Midnight is Media Nox,
The hour of logic and science,
The consideration of probabilities.
Midnight: a dirt road between
Bloomfield and Albuquerque
Here, Willa Cather wrote
'The earth is the floor of the sky'.
From grass rippling in wind,
To the moonstruck upper air:
A hundred miles of atmosphere
In one glimpse.

*

Dusk is Obscurum et Crepusculum,
The hour of mystery,
Art's obsessions,
The awareness of possibilities.
Dusk: the cliffs of Sedona
Burning behind a juniper screen.
Far from mystics and merchants,
An essential magic returns
Summoned not by incense
And talismans, but by
Cricket songs and the crunch
Of my shoes over red gravel.

*

Noon is Meridies
The hour of contemplatio
Serenity.
Noon: golden clay hills
In the Bisti badlands
Under Maynard Dixon's
'Blue ecstasies of air'.
After rain, pools jewel
Sandstone outcrops.
Bend to drink, and touch seashells:
The ghosts of shores
Dry for millions of years.

*

Dawn is Diluculum et Prima Lux
The hour of awakening,
The welcome realization of change.
Dawn: an artesian spring
Below the Mogollon Rim,
Its shape echoing Spanish fountains,
The quest for seven cities of gold.
Treasure can be as simple as
A rock to rest upon,
And morning after long night.

Hundred Mile River

2006

From cloud-veiled granite scarps,
Seven springs flow toward the sunset:
Icy ripples on darkening stone,
Braided silver through grassy flats,
Already muddied, mined, dyed red with rust,
They join.
One stream settles in a green bowl where
A prim town smoothes its skirts,
Locomotives climb up the valley bearing
Summer pilgrims: miners, loggers, tourists,
Mystics who watch the bitter current
Coil south without them.
A narrow river cleansed with a thousand streams,
Aquamarine under sunlight, gliding blue-black
Under storm,
Poisoned more than once
By autumn-yellow mine tailings.
Curtains of pine and pink rock set the stage
For marvels: a double rainbow, three trout
Jump in unison, the great rapids bloom in
Furious white,
Lightning fuses a sandbank
Into rings of glass.
A dozen channels etch the glacial floor
With oxbow flourishes, unconstrained

Calligraphy around campgrounds,
Gingerbread houses, the obligatory mall,
Jade sluices where kayakers play under
A four-lane bridge.
Pines vanish into golden grass and juniper,
Raven-haunted cliffs, long miles cobbled with
Glacier-rounded stones:
Under the carpet of cottonwoods,
In marshes flickering with carp, this valley
Remembers run-off from a million winters.
The last thirteen miles run through
Orchards and junkyards,
Limping, sullen with silt, too exhausted
To fight confluence
A thread of brown water
Mingling with clean blue,
Subsumed into its tamed sister.
Did the river die here, or back
On the polluted mountain?
What difference does it make
To one water molecule
Or a trillion,
Borne once again toward
Sea and cloud?

Blessing of the Multitudes

2000

Summer blows into floating golden leaves.
The sun and I walk
Southwest from the river.
Shallow water braids through dry sand,
Murmuring 'come spring!'
Threats to deadwood.
I won't see spring along the Rio de las Animas.
One of me won't see spring again.
She whispers to me:

[You need to go away soon.]

Wind bends yellow wheat in the valley,
Skims junipers and red rocks,
Scatters oak leaves through ancient ruins,
Scours dust from the highways
That all lead away.

[You could go to Rochester.]

I don't go to Rochester.
What would I do in a land so green
I can't see dirt?
Who is that girl, anyway?
She has a full scholarship.
I toyed with prisms for one semester.

I can't remember the paper they said I wrote.
I can't remember stealing it, either.

    So maybe one of us wrote it.

She knows optics and Lake Effect snow.
In a decade or two she works on
A new telescope in Chile.
We are all tetrachromats:
She moonlights for color designers,
Fidgets with a gemstone spectrum
On a silver chain.
I've made one like it:
Amethyst, iolite, tourmaline, citrine,
Carnelian, and garnet.
Before the internet, we all
Collected travel brochures
Books on faraway places.

    No place far enough

From this dusty land, soon
Three shades of winter brown.
I can't spend another winter here.

    But I do.

As far as the nearest town,
A big white college:
Layer-cake buildings spilling
Over northern hills,
All that knowledge,
That library and its gallery.
Its rituals:

Ten thousand farolitos
Glowing in December dusk.
Stoop, light one, stand,
Shuffle to the next,
Feet freezing in their boots,
The price for Belonging.

    Until I don't belong anymore.

I have a degree,
Why should I want to stay?
I want to stay.
Summer's ghost is still
Breathing in my ear:
Where are my white hot silver hills?
The green cottonwoods
A mossy froth over
Red stone switchbacks
Shawled with rain clouds,
Gasoline fumes, clotted with
Neon tourists?
Towers of peach thunderheads
And pink lightning?
Spirals of crows playing
Over a one-street downtown?

    In the space of two weeks,
    Gold trees dim under blue steel sky.

There's another girl as obsessed
With silver as Rochester and I,
She just wants it more.
I catch dream-glimpses of her art

In New York galleries,
Museums, glossy magazines.
Some of my best work
Approaches her worst.

      Do any of them wonder

About me?
Do I ever do anything worth
Looking across the universes?
The last week at home:
Willow canes turn their shoulders
To the sun,
Scant leaves penning messages
On red wine clouds.

      [A decade before Columbine,
      One of us has a shotgun
      And a high-school grudge.
      Look aside from her.]

There is a boy, a car, and a job.
I know how this goes, how this will go
For thirty years, down in
Shimmering desert.

      I go anyway.

Thirty years of laughter. Tears.
Our tracks are splitting
Toward different infinities.
He has his own multitudes.

      Stay. Go. Follow my summer.

Follow my million sibling-selves
Across the multiverse.

    [Do anything.]

I say that to the one still walking
By the Animas,
Under golden cottonwoods.
She dreams of blue trees
And black lightning,
Another multiverse
Budding inside her.
She loves it
More than Rochester.
More than silver.

    We want to see where she goes.

The City Revealed

2017

Beyond a purple twilit plain,
A city revealed and concealed
By sunset and slanting rain:
Its shadowed stairs, amber towers,
Floating banners, garden bowers
Amid drifts of smoke and plaintive song
To some splendid state belong...
All echoes in the hollow ruin
Unmasked by a later, colder moon.

Night Flight

2015

Earth rolls east from sunset.
Below this hill,
The City embarks nightward,
Trailing jewels and fire.

Jade Buttons

2005

Two jade buttons
Clasp silken sleeves
Around sturdy wrists
Under white fur robes
Against winter night
On the pine-clad hills
Of the Iron Tiger's kingdom.
You are the price for your village.
What price will you pay,
Sunbird's child
To tarry here in
Moonstone midnights
And the warmth
Of a dangerous lover?
When he undoes the
Green jade holding
The silk to your skin,
Will he find the
Small bronze knife?

The Frog and The Moon

1996

A frog fell in love with the Moon.
He climbed a tall reed and sang to her,
But she walked across the sky without stopping.
A hungry owl heard the song and flew down.
The Moon stepped from behind the clouds.
Blinded by sudden light, the owl's strike missed.
Safe again in his lake, the frog knew
That the Moon knew
He loved her.
But he never climbed so high again
Knowing also the Moon's moods
Like her light,
Were bright, dark, and ever-changing.

Permafrost

2004

Hold back early spring:
Frozen brown earth
Traps ancient poisons.

Green Desert

2002

In an oasis of illusion

    (Golf course, adobe wall)

In citadels of sand

    (Xeriscape, shopping mall)

Too many dreamy pilgrims

    (Fashion show, traffic crawl)

Trespass a fragile land.

    (Infill, urban sprawl)

The Christmas Mix

1999

In the dry brown winter of 1975, I learned that I was part-Native on my father's side, and therefore had a vague cultural right to scour my school playground in search of anything suitably Indigenous.

To untrained eyes, old lineoleum tile can resemble potsherds. I was untrained, said the docents at our local museum, but I got approval for my enthusiasm.

A gigantic and genuinely-famous cottonwood tree anchored one corner of the playground. It had sheltered and tantalized generations of schoolchildren. Between its knotted roots and twisted bark-crevasses, I found tiny bits of glass colored blue, green, red, and white: beads!

I knew about beads from television shows and magazine stories about the Tutankhamen Exhibition touring North America.

I was more interested in the beads than in playing with my classmates.

We didn't know the word 'autistic' in 1975.

My fifth-grade teachers called it 'antisocial behavior'.

I called it 'thing-finding', after a game from the Pippi Longstocking books. My mom, when she realized why I was excavating Park Avenue Elementary School's back lot instead of socializing with my peers, called it 'practical archaeology' and gave me my first public library card.

"Well," she asked me a few weeks later. "What have you found?"

"Beads," I said.

"How old are they?"

I squinted at one bead. I hadn't washed it, and its hole was packed solid with old dirt. I consulted a library book about northern New Mexico. Wincing at the desecration, I chipped one striped sky-blue bead with a pair of pliers. Glass beads, not painted pottery or turquoise. So much for Anasazi Indian treasure-troves, Mayan artifacts, or other mementos from the distant past. "New beads, probably," I sighed.

"How new?"

I thought about it over dinner. "I didn't dig much, they were on the surface. The school was built in the 1950s, right?" In the middle of mashed potatoes and Salisbury steak, I bolted for my mom's hoard of National Geographic magazines, and looked carefully at the jewelry advertisements from that prehistoric decade. I saw strings of pearls, silver poodles and golden teddy bears with 'genuine Diamondite eyes!', and wispy little gold pins of carved jade leaves and ivory flowers. No mixed solid color beads, or the latest prize: round blue seed-beads striped with chipmunk brown and tan along their sides.

We drove out to the nearest Anasazi ruins, my hometown's pride and glory, and for once I bypassed the empty pueblo in favor of the tourist trap/trading post. The stock was always the same: beef jerky and cactus candy, expensive turquoise jewelry and cheap plastic pop-guns. Plus a million little glass beads, strung in necklaces, sewn on western shirts and leather moccasins, and glued to cow skulls.

I spilled a few of my beads on the counter. "You ever sell anything like these, mister?"

The owner humored me, and looked. Then he checked a wholesale catalog—a revelation to me.

There were places *that just sold beads*?

I borrowed his catalog, and wrote away for others. The trail splintered into equal parts of fantasy and history, as I learned more: had Spanish explorer Juan Maria de Rivera carried trade beads north on his survey of the Colorado River Basin? Did a Victorian lady buy them in Italy, or a fur-trader use them as currency? Were they lost by a hippie girl, just a few years before I found them?

I never learned.

Before I knew there were other beaders who might help me research, I gave those treasured beads away to a dear friend moving overseas.

Years afterward, while living in Phoenix, Arizona, I wandered into a huge bead store and saw a wall of striped and solid-colored glass beads. Some were ancient and very valuable 'trade' pieces worth hundreds of dollars for one bead. Others were new, smaller, simpler, and affordable. I loved the six-foot-long loops of small mixed beads, for $1 a strand. 'The Christmas Mix', the store owner called them, because they looked like holiday garlands. I bought five of them.

On a later trip back to my hometown, after my mother had died the summer before, I wore those five necklaces over my sweater when I visited the weekend-deserted school playground.

The buildings were different, and some of the old cottonwood trees were gone. The giant tree was fenced off, too unsafe for children to play under. But the dirt lot was the same—scuffed, hard-packed, winter-dry, a blank surface hiding untold treasures.

I reached up with a pair of embroidery scissors and snipped all the strands at once.

With beads pattering like multicolored rain off my shoulders, I walked away, whispering, "Merry Christmas!" to the next thing-finder.

Cottonwood Rituals

2020

On cold grey March days
Cottonwood resin began to rise
In the tangle of trees along the southern fence
Of a tan and gray-green school
Fossilized in 1954.

*

Amber droplets edged leaf buds.
Sweetness bee-harvested
To line hives with antiseptic wax;
A balm I learned to brew from
Family folktales of a grandmother
Gone before I was born.
April's green was long weeks away.

*

Resin drops fell under spreading branches,
Sticky brown tar awaiting unwary bullies,
Terpenes weathering through sun and summer
On the pink clay ground.

*

When leaves turned September's gold
Resin fragments looked like rusted garnet,

Smelling sharp and sweet.
Gathered,
Washed,
Turning pliable and perfumed
Warmed by my hands,
A primeval plastic
Sealing basket weaves
Gluing turquoise chips to wood carvings
Sculpting tiny red talismans:
Greek horses, Gothic crowns, filigreed lotus,
Secret keys, and ancient runic tablets
Pressed with fingernails and pencils
While the homeroom teacher wasn't watching.

*

The scent still centers me
Fifty years later.

Prairie Skies (Eastern Colorado)

2007

I have only seen that sapphire blue
Just east of zenith
In the shadow of a thunderhead
Three hours before sunset.
Stand twenty miles away and look
Up through sliding layers of cloud
Sun-silvered anvils bracket the sky,
In their skirts
Glints of lightning promise rain.
Under the storm rears a long mountain
At the mountain's gold-grass verge
Highrises crouch, glass canyons
Vibrate with human pulses,
A shimmering nightscape woven
Into dreams and nightmares.
Look east from the city!
Before the mountain roll vast plains
Between two worlds and the curved horizon.
Sage smell in the air
Below the cliffs a river cuts through time
This land bears the stamp of geology,
Of ages.
Some vistas linger best in memory.
How can you not see this?
The wind and the grass have seen it all before.

Radio Silence

1990

I got stuck in a class that I couldn't pass
Because of boredom
With a teacher who thought science fiction was sin.
One day I back-talked the local jock
He turned around and said:
"Hey, Miss Spock, I liked you better
When you were quiet and shy."
I said, "I'm not shy.
I'm on radio silence behind enemy lines,
Sorting truth from the lies, a deep cover spy
On alien minds.
You go your way and I'll go mine
There really isn't a grand design
It's nothing personal, just radio silence."
I got stuck with a stint at the party
To end all parties,
Enjoying the scene but knowing I didn't fit in,
When a talent scout looked me up
And looked me down.
Saying, "Honey, you could help your career
If you weren't so shy."
And I said,
"I'm not shy.
I'm on radio silence behind enemy lines,
Sorting truth from the lies, a deep cover spy

On alien minds.
You go your way and I'll go mine
There really isn't a grand design
It's nothing personal, just radio silence."
Now there are people you meet
Out in the street in the daytime
Who might be gifted but they won't channel Isis for you.
As far as it goes they've got one goal:
Keeping together body and soul.
It's nothing personal,
Just radio silence.

Oceania

1990

I learned to sail when I was nine,
Had an ocean-going tri hull
By the time I was seventeen
And now I have seen
The Isle of Glass like a beacon
On the horizon line.

    She isn't ours anymore, she's Oceania
    She isn't Earth anymore, she's Oceania.

They said the sea might never rise.
She drowned the coasts in sixty years,
Now otters play where banners flew
And lights filled the skies.

    She isn't ours anymore, she's Oceania
    She isn't Earth anymore, she's Oceania.

Dream In Color

1995

An artist touted brown and ashen drawings:
Twisted trees and Fae deermaidens
Anchoring a thousand incense stores,
Wringing pale hands on creamy notecards,
Pouting, primly invoking Yeats:
'I have spread my dreams under your feet,
Tread softly.'

*

Stomp grapes over your dreams.
Carry gem-colored corncobs in them,
Muddy from autumn fields.
Carry gold nuggets plucked in
Icy streams below mountains glowing
Blue-silver under moonlight.
Carry your own heart,
Torn out,
Still pulsing.

*

If dreams are such fragile cobwebs
They cannot withstand use,
Then poets and magicians must
Loom stronger stuff.

Dance to wilder drums,
Take a deeper drink of Hippocrene,
Aim the arrow, but having
Aimed, let go!
'For you tread upon my dreams.'

*

The artist did not
Quote more:
'If I had the Cloths of Heaven—'

*

Remember this reason for
The Silk Road's fame:
Samarkand's paper wove an
Empire of poetry and science.
Carpets are but the floor of dreams:
Trod upon
Prayed upon,
Danced upon,
Flown upon
Over earth and time.
I make magic carpets,
And I dream in color.

Continental Divide

2004

From here I cannot see two oceans.
Standing astride this ridge, one foot
Touching sunset
The other, night.
On each side, cool winds taste the same.
From here I see no difference between
Factory or farm, trailer or mansion,
No hint of hand or ideology behind
The lights that in distant valleys bloom.
Thrumming roads, the tight hives of towns,
Diamond cities spilled across the dark...
All nerves flooded by two signals,
Twin prayers voiced and un-uttered.
From here I see only the twilight,
And I recall how Church
Painted Cotopaxi in the shadow
Of Civil War.

The Truth Remains

2002

Ignore the truth
Forget the name
Rewrite the history
Erase the word
Silence the voice
Destroy the haven
Pass the blame
The truth remains

A Thing Created

2000

There are misers
In shadowed hallways
Who never learn the simple truth
Of glory's price
A thing created
Carries magic
To the moment
We deem it done.
From that moment,
It leaves our keeping,
Whether we hold it fast
Or let it fly.
There will always be other
Enchantments to weave,
Always fire in the soul.
Holding on only leads us to grieve,
The letting go keeps us whole.

Prayer For Rain

2000

Land, air, and ocean form
An interlocking chain.
For every coastline scarred by storm,
A heartland prays for rain.

Narrow Shore

2015

We are fortunate.
Our desert is not yet on fire.
Four hundred miles east of the flames
Our noon sky is sullen turquoise
Over a land of broken jasper.
Under rusted sunlight,
Shadows are green as old bruises,
Not the clean sharp lapis of decades past.

*

The night casts drab murks
Across dim stars, sulphuric moons,
Airplanes that must seem
Marooned above this monstrous haze,
Departing and arriving within the same
Sagasso continent of acrid fog.
Jacaranda and yucca bloom feverishly
A month earlier than twenty years ago,

*

Buds browned at the edges,
Scorched perfume too faint to entice
Starving moths waiting out the smoke.
Broken black feathers tangle in tumbleweed:

Young grackles foundered at first flight.

*

Everywhere, we hear the Doom Bell:
Storm, drought, and fire its harbingers
Not of Collapse but worse.
A Change that no longer favors us.
We wasted ten thousand years,
A racial childhood now lost to Entropy.

*

Everywhere, we hear the Doom Bell.
Recognising danger,
Projecting onto easy targets.
The quick fix, isn't.
We comfort ourselves in dwindling routine,
Banal laughter over silent fear.
All systems strain toward Reset.
Heed the geometry of psychosis,
The symmetry of compassion.
Reality trumps resentment.
The universe's greatest Secret:
It does not care.

*

So we must learn from scattered feathers
The augury of new worlds
Before they come true.

*

Each year the universe pulls away.
Each year it darkens as the first light fades.
Heroes saw the Earth from space.
Their thoughtless children
Forgot the urgent stars.
Drowned out the tolling bell,
Ignored the closing door.
Until trapped along this narrow shore
Between the howling desert
And the rising deep:
Too weak to endure,
Too spent to leap.

Lie of the Land

2020

Under two centuries of sunlight
Shards of clear glass have burned
The amethyst of winter twilights
Or days-distant mountains.
From the road this land seems nearly pristine,
Our oldest traces smoothed by wind and snow.
The road twists, branching between mesas,
Arrowing into distance.
From three miles up, the Colorado Basin is a lacework
Of coyote paths to ruins and vanished ranchos.
The oilfield stamp of line-and-terminus:
A manuscript vine or circuit board
Etched along the topography of ancient carbon.
Every mile crowded with old wells still ticking meters.
Brown oil and simmering gas driving
Myths of manifest destiny
Or abandoned, cement-plugged cenotaphs
Of caustics pumped underground
Trapping ghosts of Paleozoic swamps
And 1950s roughnecks still remembering
The AM radio bounced down from Denver
Or the taste of blackberry pie.
The high desert I knew as a child
Is not the land of the Anasazi
Or even the orchard-planters of the 1890s.

Tumbleweed and Russian olive
Strangled the willow meadows,
Ploughs broke the cottonwood groves.
Drought is changing the land again,
Juniper and pinon dying off,
Even the alien grasses fade
Into unknown futures.

Artist's Invocation

1985

All glories I have wrought
By hand and gift of seeing,
All dreams I have brought
From dreamscape into being,
All lessons I have learned
By choice or chance meeting,
Mingle in the truth I've sought:
Streams at the sea, completing.

Wait

1985

At sunset, we drink
An ancient wine.
Stars rise in
The indigo east.
A clean winter wind
Scatters memories
Like leaves
Across the snow.
In firelight, glass
Rings in a crystal sigh
For lives etched in
Eyes and silver hair.
As the wind brings a
Scent of far-off spring,
Each breathes: 'Wait.
I'll meet you there.'

Afterword

Thank you for reading this shamelessly-personal journey back into a few of my collected notes, stories, and poems from the last thirty-five years.

Many of my poems are actually songs I sang, or were originally embroidered or painted as the central texts in one-of-a-kind fiber and bead artists' books. You can see more of my art at the 'Art' section of my website at www.cranehanabooks.com.

'The Blood Orange Tree' was published in a slightly-different form in 2000, in the Meisha-Merlin SFF anthology *Such A Pretty Face: Tales of Power and Abundance.*

'The Christmas Mix' appeared in slightly different form in *Bead & Button Magazine #34,* December 1999.

Cover design by Marian Crane. Cover art 'Storm Jewel', copyright 2009 by Marian Crane

About the Author

As M. Crane Hana, I write erotic romance, high fantasy, and space fantasy.

As Marian Crane, I'm known for jewelry design, book sculpture, and fiber arts.

As Filigree, I make trouble online.

Read more at https://www.cranehanabooks.com.